MW00881056

i

Sacred Moments

Prayers of a Navy Chaplain
at Sea and Ashore

Volume I: Prayers at Sea: Destroyer
Squadron Fifteen (CDS 15) and
USS PELEIU (LHA 5)

Paul W. Murphey

Create Space
2013

Copyright 2013 Paul W. Murphey
All rights reserved
ISBN13: 978-1482639575
ISBN10:1482639572

North Charleston, SC:
Create Space, 2013

Dedicated with deepest gratitude to
Captain Thomas P. Scott,
USN (Retired)
Commanding Officer, USS PELELIU
(LHA 5), 1980-1982

Even before he knew who his chaplain would be he welcomed him and made him a vital part of an incredible team of officers and men dedicated to nothing less than their absolute best following his leadership and example.

Contents

Preface

Sacred moments often come to us unexpectedly. They open us to the reality of the divine presence in our ordinary experiences. At other times we prepare for them as best we can hoping and praying that what we say or do may somehow make us and others more aware that God has created us in His image so that we might live creatively, responsibly, lovingly. We know them in our successes when we live a life of gratitude. But, sometimes to our amazement we know them in our failures when we have done our best and things still have not worked out as we had planned.

They may come to us at the beginning of our day when we first awake and get started with what lies ahead. They may meet us anywhere along the way not just in the still silences of our waiting but even in the busy rush of a schedule more crowded than we had anticipated. They await us when we lie down to sleep and pray for untroubled rest and much needed renewal.

A Navy Chaplain is called to be a visible reminder of life's sacred moments. Nowhere is this more evident than when he or she is given the privilege of leading men and women in prayer. For a Chaplain at sea the most sacred moment of the day is the Evening Prayer which is offered to God on behalf of the crew over the

1 MC -- the ship's main internal communications system. In the silent darkness as he stands off the bridge and invites those who can to pause with him for the Evening Prayer, he cannot see them but knows from things they have said to him that they are listening and that the prayers do indeed become sacred moments for many of them. It is not just the openly religious but others one might never expect who find meaning and value in those moments. The prayers should have universal inclusion of all the crew while at the same time being specific enough that each crewman finds him-self once again aware of living in God's presence.

I had at first intended to publish only Evening Prayers at Sea but became conscious that any prayer may become a sacred moment. The endeavor was expanded to include prayers on other occasions ashore as well as at sea. I regret that many prayers were not written down and saved so cannot appear here. The list is long even when they are edited to compress space thus making it seem better to issue them in three small volumes.

Since Evening Prayers are the most vivid expression of sacred moments, at least for this retired Navy Chaplain, they appear first. The first volume covers my first two sea assignments: COMDESRON FIFTEEN (CDS 15) and USS PELELIU (LHA 5).   Two non-consecutive tours as Command Chaplain on USS MIDWAY (CV 41) provided enough prayers for a separate volume. Shore duty was first chronologically as I served at a Naval and Marine Corps Reserve Center in Lexington, Kentucky while living and working as a professor in a university setting. However those prayers appear in the third volume since they are more akin to prayers in a civilian setting. It was Active Duty at Sea that made me aware that the prayers I offered were in more ways than I had imagined truly sacred moments.

I am deeply grateful to all the men and women with whom I was privileged to serve in the U.S. Navy. I thank God for opening to me a world far greater than I had dreamed of. Life as a College Professor was grandly satisfying but life in the Navy taught me lessons about humanity I could never have learned there. My life was enriched immeasurably and blessed by God as I shared the joys and sorrows, hopes and fears, dreams and disappointments of human beings of indescribable diversity who let me become a part of their lives simply because I was their Chaplain.

I will try to use names circumspectly and never refer to anyone in a way that would identify him or her in a demeaning or dehumanizing manner. Regrettably not all those who played a tremendously positive role in my being able to serve others can or will be named.

I mean no slight to those not named. It is just that I do not want these three volumes to become a memoir so much as a setting for the Sacred Moments of a Navy Chaplain in his prayers at sea and ashore.

This first volume is dedicated to Captain Thomas P. Scott, USN (Retired) who was the first Commanding Officer of USS PELELIU (LHA 5). He was any Chaplain's dream. Even before the Ship was Commissioned he designated the stateroom adjacent to his in-port cabin as the Chaplain's stateroom.

Before we set sail on our maiden voyage he had the engineers fabricate a brass plaque with a PELELIU medal and a St. Michael's medallion with the words: *Let this be a perpetual reminder of faith in God by whose grace we, the men of USS PELELIU, devote ourselves to the extraordinary accomplishment of every mission.* This was affixed to the ship's direction indicator on the bridge as a constant reminder of the significance of our service. He was a truly remarkable leader and a devout Roman Catholic who never missed Mass whenever we could have a priest aboard to celebrate it.

What is published in these volumes is in no way to be construed as expressing an official position of the US Navy and particularly of the Chaplain Corps. To the best of my knowledge when specific events or incidents are referred to no breach of secrecy or violation of privacy has occurred. The events are far enough in the past that they would not disclose even inadvertently information unavailable to a conscientious researcher.

These are the experiences and reflections of one particular chaplain; other chaplains might have or have had similar experiences but each performs his or her duties consistent with his or her abilities, calling, and commitment. I have usually used the masculine form because that was my experience. The Navy is now fortunate in having capable women Chaplains as well as Chaplains from faiths beyond Christian and Jewish.

Introduction

This book of prayers of a Navy Chaplain expresses one particular Chaplain's offerings to God on behalf of the people with whom he was privileged to serve. Other Chaplains would have, and did, express themselves differently. The prayers are often like a log or journal entry of what was happening at that time within the Command and sometimes beyond. Through them even a person who has never been to sea may be able to catch a glimpse of what life at sea was like at the time the prayers were given.

The life of a Navy Chaplain at sea is unique among forms of ministry. The Chaplain lives and works with his congregation in the narrow confines of the ship twenty-four hours a day, seven days a week. Chaplains ashore like their civilian counterparts are able to become as close or as distant from their parishioners as their personalities and sense of calling and the propensities of their people allow.

In the civilian pastorate a minister is known primarily for his sermons and pastoral care. A Navy Chaplain soon learns that while he should be conscientious about sermon preparation and delivery, he will not be known for his preaching prowess. That is why I have focused on prayers as the most sacred moments of a Navy Chaplain.

In a Base Chapel a Chaplain may preach to hundreds; at sea that will probably never be the case. When in port he will go aboard his ship or ships equipped to lead in worship and deliver appropriate sermons. There will be days when there may only be two or three crewmen; even some days when no one shows up after the word is passed that religious services are being held on the mess-deck, foc'sile, or in the ship's chapel if there is one. On those occasions he will make use of that time to visit with some of the duty section sharing his concern and care for them as a visible symbol of God's generous love for all of us.

In a shore assignment a Chaplain may be able to fulfill his duties by attending to the distinct dimensions of ministry with which he is already familiar. Preaching, performing weddings, counseling those who come to him, teaching about the faith, visiting the sick, and ministering to the dying and bereaved will regularly be engaged in. In a sea-going command, especially a command with limited staff he may be tasked with several "additional duties" such as Educational Services Officer, Library Officer, Navy Relief Liaison, auditor of recreation funds, Project Handclasp Coordinator, Morale and Welfare Officer, Tour

Guide, advisor to Navy Spouse groups and Ombudspersons to mention a few.

The Chaplain seriously plans for and engages in a ministry of presence both at sea and ashore. He cannot wait in his office for men or women to come to him, though many will seek him or her out. He should be as familiar with the work and play spaces of his command and the persons he finds there as with the places of worship or counseling. The more visible he or she is the more likely the crew will avail themselves of his ministry to and with them. Whether at sea or ashore the chaplain will regularly lead or facilitate Bible Studies and other religious education experiences as well as pre-marriage seminars and self-awareness groups.

He will sometimes be asked to reenlist a crew member or deliver the prayers at a retirement, to help crewmen or their families resolve pay problems or settle family disputes. He will regularly visit the sick and assist crewmen in caring for their families. He will deliver far more Red Cross messages about problems at home including illness and death than he would like and will assist in arranging for emergency leave. He will attend XOIs (Executive Officer's Investigations) when Sailors face disciplinary issues and will be present at Captains Mast whenever his Commanding

Officer deems that part of his service to him and the crew. He will visit the Brig, whether on board or ashore, caring for the men of the command who have been confined there.

At sea the days and nights can run together with little to separate them, especially on a large ship like an aircraft carrier. Chaplains who appreciate this situation will become almost as familiar with sick-bay, the galley, the engine rooms, the signal bridge, the bridge itself and most other parts of the ship as with his office spaces or the small chapel or classroom where religious services are conducted.

The Chaplain is fortunate in having specially trained enlisted personnel known as Religious Program Specialists who enable him to perform the services expected of him.

He will consider his relationship with the Command Master Chief a special and privileged one as they each seek to make life better for the ship as a whole and crew members who especially need their help. His ability to help the crew-- officers and enlisted -- meet their needs and become ever more aware that we are all created in the image of God is dependent on his acceptance as a member of the team especially by the Commanding Officer and the Executive Officer.

A person becomes a Navy Chaplain only after successfully applying for commissioning as an officer in the Navy while at the same time being endorsed by a recognized ecclesiastical body. That usually means he or she has completed theological seminary after receiving his or her bachelor's degree and served at least two years in a parish church.

Once accepted either in the Reserves or on Active Duty he or she is under the care and supervision of his Endorsing Agent. That usually means regular correspondence, submission of reports and usually an annual on-site visit by his faith group's Endorsing Agent. If, for any reason, the endorsing body lifts his endorsement he can no longer serve as a Chaplain. He may request continuation of naval service but in another community such as the Supply Corps if he is qualified. There is no guarantee of continuation. There is some movement between Reserve and Active Duty components though many chaplains serve their entire Chaplaincy in one or the other. Reserve and Active Duty Chaplains serve under similar but different laws and regulations.

A Chaplain by the nature of the position must live and work well in two worlds – the world of a Naval Officer and the world of an ordained minister responsible to God and the faith community that endorses him. Literally, he must find a way to serve God and country.

Similarly he has a dual relationship to his Commanding Officer and the next highest level of supervision from the Chaplain of the type commander. For example, if he is chaplain on an amphibious ship he will serve under the supervision of the Amphibious Group Chaplain, the Surface Force Chaplain, and the Fleet Chaplain. This need not be confusing but navigating it must be learned. He must keep in mind that the Navy has "detailed" him to serve in a particular billet and his primary loyalty is to the Commanding Officer of that billet. He will, if he is wise, learn to respond appropriately to the guidance of his supervisory chaplains.

Though a Chaplain is in the naval service in part due to his ecclesiastical body's endorsement he or she is expected to be Chaplain to the entire command to which he is attached. Even if the word ecumenical is not basic in his religious affiliation as it is for some, the Chaplain is expected to minister to any and all members of the Command regardless of rate or rank, ethnicity, religious affiliation or lack thereof, gender or anything else that might artificially distinguish one person from another.

If he wishes to minister particularly to his faith group whether Roman Catholic, Jewish, Pentecostal or whatever he or she will conduct services according to the rites and regulations of that group. But, in all other ministerial functions he or she will serve all personnel and their families alike. He is at his best when he provides religious expressions for as many as choose to avail themselves of the opportunity. He does this in part through training and equipping lay leaders for specific faith expressions and facilitating time and space for those expressions.

A Chaplain is expected to be a person of integrity and do nothing intentionally which would violate the commitment he or she has to God and the religious body that has endorsed him or her.

Every person on active duty and often retirees or veterans has access to government facilities such as chapels for weddings or memorials. That does not, however, entitle them to the services of a specific Chaplain. Each Chaplain, according to his religious affiliation and personal beliefs and convictions decides what services, which are not Command functions, he or she will perform.

Knowing and understanding the vocational dimensions of ministry is essential for understanding the role the Chaplain plays in the Navy. Whether he is minister, priest, or rabbi he performs similar functions to those he performed in civilian life – preaching, teaching, counseling, administrative duties, conducting the rites and ceremonies of his faith group in matters of life and death, including weddings and funerals.

As a Navy Chaplain he is expected to be an expert in his field just as every other Department Head is in his field. Regardless of rank he is to uphold the highest standards of performance in his arena as they do in theirs whether operations, engineering, or the other vital areas of naval life at sea or ashore.

One of the first things he learns from the first at sea command to which he is assigned is that both symbols of his collar devices are important. The crew wants to know whether the religious symbol is for real – first, is he a man of faith and commitment and second, how much power does he have when needed to use on his behalf in terms of his rank.

His promotions are largely though not entirely dependent on the fitness reports he receives from his Commanding Officer. The selection to the next highest rank is by a Navy-wide board convened for that purpose. Even stellar performance with highest marks and numerous commendations does not guarantee that the Board will select him for promotion. He may know both the joy of recognition and the bitter sorrow of rejection. He is expected to perform his ministry faithfully even if "passed over" so long as he is retained as a Navy Chaplain.

While this book and the volumes that follow focus on prayers as sacred moments, these prayers will be more meaningful if those reading them have some context for understanding and appreciating their purpose and meaning. As I said earlier I have tried to avoid turning these volumes into a Memoir. However, sharing with the reader some of what was happening to me and around me as a Chaplain in a given assignment seems desirable, even necessary.

It will be evident that some basic concepts and beliefs pervade what is offered through the prayers. Most basic is a firm conviction that God is love and has created men and women in His image to be creative, loving, and responsible. Life is a journey; we are sent into time and space by birth and this particular journey culminates in death. I believe God would not create human beings simply to destroy them; so death is an ending but not the end.

There is belief in the first three axioms of the humanities: where one stands determines what one sees, we have to go from where we are, and wherever I go there I am.

I am convinced that Jesus was right when he affirmed that to whom much is given from him much is required and that a person should make the most of what he or she has been given.

I hold close two teachings I found in Nicholas Berdyaev: "we are co-creators with God of our destiny," and "life is both a gift and an achievement."

I believe also that life should be lived with gratitude and one should accept responsibility for the exercise of his freedom so far as the situation or circumstances will allow.

I think the most succinct answer to the question of when life is worth living was provided by Joseph Fort Newton when he said, "Life is worth living when I have a self fit to live with, a work fit to live for, someone to love and be loved by." How fortunate we are when these align in a satisfying and fulfilling life.

This is only an introductory glimpse into my perceptions of the life and work of a Navy Chaplain but perhaps will be enough to make the prayers which follow come alive as sacred moments once again.

Chapter I.
Destroyer Squadron Fifteen (CDS 15), Yokosuka, Japan, June, 1976-March, 1978.

A. "Not a job but an Adventure"

On Thursday I turned in my grades to the Registrar and left behind my career as a college professor. For five years I had been College Chaplain at Eureka College, Illinois. After that for eleven years I taught at Transylvania University, Lexington, Kentucky. When I set out on the new adventure of Active Duty Navy life I was a tenured full Professor and Head of the Interdisciplinary Humanities Program. In addition to teaching, among other things I had been Director of the Institutional Self-study. Now I was leaving it all behind.

I boarded a plane the next morning and with my cumbersome foot locker, large hanging suit-bag, and a bulky, oversized, rigid brief case was headed for Japan. When I had been accepted on Active Duty from the Reserves I was already 44 years old and thought I would be assigned somewhere where my academic background and Ph.D. would be put to use. Instead I received orders to report to Commander Destroyer

Squadron Fifteen home-ported in Yokosuka, Japan.

After a long series of flights from Lexington to San Francisco and San Francisco to Honolulu I landed at Haneda Airport in Tokyo. The person who was meeting me there and I failed to connect so I caught a military bus to Yokota Air Force base and spent my first night in Japan there somewhat bewildered by this exotic land which I had only heard of and read about. The next day, 14 June, 1976, I was on a military bus to Yokosuka where I reported in to COMDESRON Fifteen and began what the Navy was calling in its recruiting slogan, "Not a Job but an Adventure." That certainly proved true!

The Squadron Commodore and Staff had offices ashore and embarked either as a unit or for individual assignments aboard ship as needed.

The ships of the Squadron were USS PARSONS (DDG 33), USS BAUSELL (DD 845), USS FRANCIS HAMMOND (FF 1067), USS KIRK (FF 1087). USS LOCKWOOD (FF 1064), USS KNOX (FF 1052) was reassigned from Pearl Harbor to Yokosuka and joined the Squadron in 1977.

Whenever I was in-port Yokosuka and we had one or more ships there I went aboard each ship prepared to hold a worship service.

There were several times when five of the ships were in-port at the same time and I visited each one. Usually there would be only two or three men. Sometimes no one would come to the announced worship service, so I would go about the ship visiting with the duty section and making by my presence and concern a visible expression of God's generous care for all of us. The words did not have to be pious or pointedly religious; the spirit of what happened had to convey appreciation, concern and openness to each of them created in God's image.

On Christmas Day 1977 I was aboard all five of the DESRON FIFTEEN ships as well as USS Rathburn (FF 1057), USS BREWTON (FF 1086), USS Dubuque (LPD 8) and USS White Plains (AFS 4).

In the prayers which follow it will be observed most of the prayers are identified with my time aboard USS PARSONS (DDG 33) and USS BAUSELL (DD 845). I regret that I am unable to locate prayers from the other ships. Many of them were not written out; obviously, those that were have been lost. There were Evening Prayers at Sea aboard the FRANCIS HAMMOND, the KIRK, the LOCKWOOD and the KNOX but I cannot find copies of those.

Much of the time aboard was spent visiting with men in their spaces. I have never known a more confining and scary space than the boiler room on the BAUSELL. There was only one small ladder down into the bowels of the ship where steam hissed and the heat was almost unbearable. I immediately gained a well-deserved respect and admiration for a ship's engineers. What a contrast with the air-conditioned engine room spaces of the more modern ships.

I was aboard each of the ships many times and would often be heloed (transported by helicopter) from one to the other without a port visit in between.

Being hoisted by the "horse collar" and then let down on the rolling deck of the receiving ship was a lesson in trust of those who knew what they were doing. As a person who had a fear of heights I soon got over that fear.

It will be noted that there are prayers aboard USS HENRY B. WILSON (DD 7). She was not part of DESRON FIFTEEN. Her homeport was San Diego and she was on a WESTPAC, a prolonged deployment to the Western Pacific. I had ridden the BAUSELL (DD 845) to Subic Bay and debarked since that ship was heading further south after maintenance and liberty. I had to find a way back to Yokosuka or to Chinhae, Korea where the Staff was at the time. The HENRY B. WILSON was going there and was kind enough to let me hitch a ride.

Another time I had ridden the PARSONS from Chinhae to Keelung in the worst storm at sea I ever experienced. I can't remember a man aboard who was not sea sick as the waves crashed over the bow and reached over the bridge. The configuration of the ship contributed to a very erratic pattern in which she would pitch to one side then snap back with a jerk. What an adventure!

I disembarked the ship when we reached Keelung since she was headed further South. I had to find a way back to Yokosuka and was able to get a ride on a US AIR FORCE plane headed for Yokota AFB, Japan sitting in the back-up seat behind the pilot.

As I say in one of the prayers on the BAUSELL that ship always made me feel at home and was as fine an introduction to life at sea as I could have had.

Commander John H. McMillan was an extraordinary leader and naval officer. Whenever I went aboard we sat down together and he asked me what my goals were for that deployment. In turn, he told me what he would like to see me accomplish for the good of the ship while I was aboard. I was cordially received by officers, chiefs and other crewmembers alike. The entire wardroom with the exception of the Commanding Officer and the Executive Officer were young enough to have been my sons. That was true of the crew with the exception of a few Chief Petty Officers. I learned so much of what a chaplain could and could not do among those remarkable men.

An important aspect of Chaplaincy is facilitating opportunities for religious expression by as many personnel as possible. One way of doing that is training and equipping lay leaders to conduct religious services on their ship. Whenever I rode a ship I spent time with the designated lay leaders including attending services which they conducted. Another way of caring for the whole crew was inviting Chaplains of other faith identifications to perform services aboard.

One of the most memorable religious services while I was with DESRON FIFTEEN was an ecumenical midnight Christmas Eve service complete with the Eucharist in the hanger bay of USS LOCKWOOD (FF 1064) in port Yokosuka. Chaplain Ed Gallagher, from the Chapel of Hope, CFAY, with whom I had a cordial personal and professional relationship stood at one end of the communion table and invited Roman Catholics to receive "the body and blood of Christ" from him; I stood at the other end of the table inviting all others to partake of the bread and the wine. The service was well attended by DESRON FIFTEEN Staff and their families as well as several men from the other ships on that beautifully clear star-lit night.

From the day I arrived at DESRON FIFTEEN I was mentored by the Command Master Chief (CMC), HTCM Ron Campagna who did everything he could to help me make a successful transition from the academic world to the Navy. No one could have been a better guide, traveling companion and colleague in every endeavor than Master Chief Campagna.

For the two Christmas seasons I was with DESRON FIFTEEN the Squadron had a fantastic celebration for the orphanages, veterans home, old folks home, and TB hospital in and around Chinhae and Masan, Korea. The Naval Reserve units in my hometown of Augusta, Georgia and from Lexington, Kentucky sent many boxes of toys and candy which we distributed. The regional Commissary Office and others provided samples and other goods for the festive occasions. The Seventh Fleet even sent their band along with us for the parade, complete with clowns, jugglers, yoyo champions and happy, smiling Sailors down Chinhae's streets.

One of the primary components of DESRON FIFTEEN"s mission at the time was assisting the South Korean Navy in training and improving mission readiness. We usually had at least one ship in Chinhae at any given time.

Through the good graces and kindness of Mr. Chong, Sam Cho who was the Chapel Administrator at Chinhae we were introduced to three orphanages which I visited each time I was in port. We also went to other places such as a Veterans' Village far away in the hills and a Tuberculosis Hospital and Old Folks home in Masan.

When a new Navy Hospital was being constructed in Yokosuka surplus beds, night stands and other furnishings were made available to us and delivered by our ships to Korea.

All the work wasn't done away from home. In Yokosuka I had the usual activities of a Chaplain including meeting with Wives Club, Ombudspersons, persons seeking counsel and guidance in resolving personal issues. That kept me well acquainted with Personnel-men, Yeomen, Disbursing Clerks, Red Cross Representatives, Navy Relief workers, hospital and brig staff, Alcohol Rehabilitation Center staff who were providing support and resources for men addicted to alcohol or drugs, and JAG (Judge Advocate General) officers. I want to share one particular situation.

A young Japanese wife and her two young children came to see me for help getting support from her former husband who had divorced her. She had tried to resolve it with his ship but he had transferred duty stations and they were unable to help her. She had also tried with the Base Legal Office but nothing had come of it. I made an appointment with the Senior JAG Officer at COMNAVFORJAPAN. She and I went to see him.

When we entered he said, "Chaplain, what in God's name are you involved in this for?" I replied, "Thank you Captain, it is in God's name that I am here to see if this lady can get the help she needs and deserves." He was cordial after that and turned the case over to a Lieutenant who resolved it to her benefit in very short order. It was one of those experiences in which I knew I had made the right decision by becoming a Navy Chaplain and thanked God for the privilege.

At DESRON FIFTEEN I had more additional duties than at any time in my career. These included but were not limited to: Human Resource Management (N2) Division Head, HRAV Program Manager, Navy Wives and Ombudsperson Liaison Officer, Oversea Family Resident Program Manager, Educational Services Officer, and Liberty Information Representative Coordinator.

When it was learned that USS KNOX (FF 1052) was to be moved from Hawaii to Yokosuka I was fortunate enough to be appointed Project Officer for the transition. Though I was adequately equipped by age and administrative experience to lead such a group I was only a Lieutenant Commander chairing a team of nine, three of whom were Navy Captains and three others Commanders. They could not have been more gracious as we worked together. The task was completed to everyone's benefit, especially the KNOX crew and their families.

Master Chief Campagna and I flew to Hawaii and met with families to prepare them for life in Japan. He and I then sailed with them conducting orientation sessions daily. It was an honor to offer the evening prayers; consequently I deeply regret not having but one of those to include in this book.

It was not all work and no play. There were Supply Corps and Navy Birthday Balls, Open Houses and informal get-togethers, Christmas parties, CDS FIFTEEN Dining-in, trips to Tokyo, Kamakura and other interesting and exciting sites.

There was a fife and drum corps called The Ancient Mariners who dressed in uniforms of the Revolutionary War period and performed patriot music of that era. I was invited to become the Group's Chaplain and had a great time doing so. Sometimes I gave prayers at the performances and on Independence Day 1977 was the narrator for their performance at the American Embassy in Tokyo.

Serving as the Chaplain of DESRON FIFTEEN was a marvelous beginning to the grand adventure which would unfold for me as a Navy Chaplain.

B. Evening Prayers at Sea
1976, 23 June USS PARSONS (DDG 33) en-route from Pusan, Korea to Yokosuka, Japan (My first evening prayer at sea).
Good evening men, this is your Chaplain. It is good to talk with you as I go about the ship. Join me now in the evening prayer.

Heavenly Father, You *are called by so many different names, yet you are one and the same. Even those whose calling of your name is but a cry of anger, desperation, or exasperation seek a power greater than their own and without realizing it acknowledge you. If we could but learn to trust you, to love You, to live with the rich resources of your divine power, we could find satisfaction and peace. Give us the ability to encourage others in their growth. Forgive us when our own insecurity causes us to berate people and abuse our positions of authority. Make us fair in our firmness and faithful in the fulfillment of work for which we are responsible.*

Jesus the Christ reminded men long ago that he who is responsible in little things can then be trusted in greater matters. Keep us from the deception that because we have little jobs to do we should do them as little people. Keep us from sloppiness for it is a cancer that eats away at integrity. Make us the kind of persons who know who we are because we know that ultimately, whether in life or in death we are yours.

Now bless, we pray, the PARSONS, her captain and crew, with peace and satisfaction in work well done and lives well lived. Amen.

1976, 24 June USS PARSONS (DDG 33).
Good evening men. This is your Chaplain. It has been a beautiful day and is a lovely evening. Following the evening prayer some of us get together on the boat deck near the Captain's gig for Bible study. We would be glad to have you join us. Would you now join me in the evening prayer.

Eternal God, like the sea, You change and move but are never exhausted. You fascinate us and charm us and we stand in awe of You. You are life itself and we seek life. Sometimes we get so confused about what we want out of life. We get tired and discouraged.

As someone else first said, "God grant us the courage to change those things we can change, the patience to accept those things we cannot change, and the wisdom to know the difference."

[Reinhold Niebuhr]

Help us to find ways to more effectively meet the needs of our ship as well as our own personal needs. Keep us from blaming others for our failure to direct our own destiny.

Oh God, You have given each of us a life uniquely our own, may we make it a life that satisfies and fulfills. Bless now this ship, the USS PARSONS. Keep us, its officers and men, in your care now and always. Amen.

1976, 25 June USS PARSONS (DDG 33).
Good evening men. This is your Chaplain. Again I invite any of you who care to join us on the boat deck for a short period of Bible study following the evening prayer. I would like also to remind you that when you are in port in Yokosuka, I will be happy to serve you and may be contacted at COMDESRON 15 office in building B-52. Now join with me in the evening prayer.

Loving Father, once again we the men of the PARSONS are grateful for the picturesque beauty of the rich blue sea and its majestic power and for the bright beauty of the warm sun.

For many of us it has been a good day. We have found reason to be proud of others in their work and satisfaction in our own. We have seen things too that disturb us. We have been reminded how important it is that we never forget that we are first and last human beings. Let us never lose our respect for other human beings for in brutalizing them we turn ourselves into beasts.

Make us men who never lose our compassion, kindness, and concern for others. Make us strong enough to accept the weakness of others. Preserve us from hatred, bitterness, and boredom.

Even if every day cannot be exciting, keep us from blindness to each day's opportunities for seeing old things in new ways.

Sustain us now by your eternal love as we come to the close of another day. We praise you, we bless you, we worship you. Amen.

1977, 11 January USS BAUSELL (DD845) en-route from Yokosuka, Japan to Subic Bay, The Philippines.

Eternal God, the rough seas have become calmer and we have once again become aware of the constant changes of life. Our lives are like the sea -- sometimes we are turbulent, wild, and restless; we even grow sick of our own upheaval. Sometimes we flow smoothly and peacefully from one shore to another. From the sea let us learn of your love -- constant, strong, and deep. Bring us to the place of faith where turbulence and calm both assure us of your eternal faithfulness. We trust you Lord; let us trust you more. Amen.

1977, 12 January USS BAUSELL (DD845).

God, there are ordinary days and there are extraordinary days. There are so many more ordinary days than extraordinary ones in a life-time. There are ordinary lives and extraordinary lives. There are so many more ordinary lives than extraordinary ones. This has been an ordinary day and we have been aware of our ordinariness. Give us, we pray, extraordinary faith to endure the ordinary while we prepare for the extraordinary events which make it all worthwhile. Help us to accept ourselves and our shipmates, ordinary as we are, because we live in your extraordinary love. Amen.

1977, 16 January USS BAUSELL (DD845).

God, what is this strange thing called religion? In your name people have murdered, warred, pillaged, and destroyed. In your name they have been cruel, stern, and judgmental. In your name they have made the sensitive suffer from an uneasy conscience while the tough-minded took advantage of their meekness and temerity. Forgive us if we have made religion an excuse for weakness rather than an affirmation of strength. Forgive us if we have hidden our own deep feelings about the goodness of life and the need to love and be loved behind a fear of being religious. Make us truly religious, Oh God, that is, enable us to live full lives as men responsible to one another because we are ultimately responsible to You, the Lord and Giver of Life. Amen.

1977, 19 January USS BAUSELL (DD845).
God, our Father, Jesus once said, "The rain falls on the just and unjust alike." We all have the same warm sun, the same bright starry night, the same changing seas. We all have only so much space on this ship. Why is it that some people steal from their shipmates whose fate is their fate and whose conditions of life are the same as theirs? We trust You God. We wish we could trust all our shipmates. But, since we can't always let us be careful to remove any temptation from those so weak or so corrupt that their evil tears down the trust so essential for living together productively. The loss of money and cameras is regrettable, but the loss of respect for one another is disastrous. Forgive us Lord. Amen.

1977, 20 January USS BAUSELL (DD845).
Eternal God, the sea tosses our small ship around like a child's boat in a bathtub as we race from point to point.

The bright sunny days we longed for are overcast by rain squalls and howling winds. Turbulence and work that never gets done disturbs our sleep. We grow weary and are eager for port. Grant us patience so that we don't become short-tempered. Calm the churning anxieties within and give us peace. Connect us to a faith which says, "peace be still for I am your God, do not be afraid, I am with you." Rest our restlessness in your eternal goodness. Amen.

1977, 21 January USS BAUSELL (DD845).
God, what can we say about a day where nothing really stands out or for which we are proud? Thank You for constant things -- for the men who prepare our food, for those who work the hot holes of boilers and engines to move us about, for those who plot our course and keep direction, for those who keep us in touch with others and us with them, and for all those whose unglamorous work makes it possible for us to live and work together on the BAUSELL. We are grateful for the constancy which makes the monotonous difficulties bearable even when there are no highs points of proud achievement. Amen.

1977, 22 January USS BAUSELL (DD845).
Eternal God, we thank You this night for calm seas. We have enjoyed the

bright warmth of the sun today and look forward to reaching port soon. We are grateful for your protection and care this cruise. We ask your blessings on those who have special needs. To those who face tests of their knowledge give alert minds and sharpened memories, to those who are afraid of their own lower desires give courage to deal with them honestly, to those who are in need of an answer to their loneliness may they find companionship rather than disillusionment. Be ever near us to make us strong. Enable us to be both responsive and responsible. Amen.

1977, 29 January USS HENRY B. WILSON (DDG7) en-route from Subic Bay, The Philippines to Chinhae, Korea.
Evening Men of USS HENRY B. WILSON. This is Chaplain Murphey. It is my pleasure to be with you. If I may share your concerns while I am aboard I would welcome the opportunity. I am in with the Engineering Officer in After Officers Quarters. Tomorrow we will have an ecumenical worship service at 0900 on the mess deck. Whether you are Protestant or Catholic, deeply or not very religious, we invite you to join us then. Now pause with me for the evening prayer.

Eternal Father, the sea is so marvelously mysterious and beautiful. She can be so calm, so peaceful, so restful and then again so wild, so turbulent, so

demanding. To sail her is a [...]
experience. Our ship is so small, t[...]
is so vast. Yet, our smallness is n[...]
insignificant for you have created us in
your image that we too might be
creative. Open us to the awareness of
your eternal presence and give to us the
joy of being co-creators worthy of being
your sons. Keep alert those who keep the
watches of the night and give to all
others rest and peace and renewal.
Amen.

1977, 30 January USS HENRY B. WILSON
(DDG 7).

Eternal God, how easy it is for us to
divide people into two groups -- the good
guys and the bad guys, friends and
enemies, saints and sinners. How easy it
is then to become self-righteously blind
to either the goodness or the need of the
other person. Maybe there is truth in the
homely saying, "there is so much good in
the worst of us, and so much bad in the
best of us that there is little reason for
any of us to talk about the rest of us." We
are glad You are not so petty and fearful
as we and that all of us depend
ultimately for our lives on your eternal
love. Help us to accept your acceptance
of us and be glad now and evermore.
Amen

rd, we trust that You
ith a sense of humor,
are trying to confess
into words the petty
the gross unspoken.
rd, from the bonds and
our offenses, real or
imag. give us for the sins we have
deliberatei, committed and forgive us
for the even greater number of
opportunities we have had to be
responsive to others' needs in your power
and have been too busy or too blind or
too careless to give of ourselves to them.
Forgive us when we have made of
religion a crutch of weakness instead of
letting our faith become a tower of
strength. Restore to us the joy of
wholeness. Free us from the bewildering
array of problems we make for ourselves.
Forgive us when we bring some
disappointment or disaster on ourselves
and then blame You by saying it is God's
will. Wake us up to your constant love
that we may live with confidence the life
which is ours through Christ. Amen.

1977, 01 February USS HENRY B. WILSON
(DDG 7).

God, sometimes religion seems so
strange, so foreign, so phony, so far away
from every day. And prayer -- what does

that have to do with the language of the mess decks, or holes or spaces? Yet, You know us better than we know ourselves. You know our cover-ups and put-ons. You know our fears and games and failures. So, we pray to communicate with You that we may see ourselves more honestly, our shipmates more as they really are and the people we meet as human beings with feelings and hopes not so different than our own. Open us to a sense of the eternal in the midst of quickly passing time, of the divine making itself known in the human. We praise You for life, your good gift. Amen.

1977, 02 February USS HENRY B. WILSON (DDG 7) approaching Chinhae, Korea. Evening Men. As you may have noticed in tomorrow's POD I am planning to visit the Chinhae Orphanages Thursday at 1330. It is always such an exciting experience and I would like you to share the joy with me. If you want to go along please sign up in the Ship's Office by noon Wednesday. Now, join me in a prayer Reinhold Niebuhr wrote as a result of his efforts as a pastor to help people of different social and economic situations to live fairly and justly with one another. It fits so many situations:

> *God give me the serenity to accept those things I cannot change,*
> *The courage to change those things I can,*

And, the wisdom to know the difference. [Reinhold Niebuhr]
May God who is able to provide for our every need bring peace and power, joy and love now and always. Amen.

1977, 14 February USS PARSONS (DDG 33) enroute from Yokosuka to Beppu, Japan.

Eternal Father, today we watched the sun-set brilliant and blazing and experienced the wonder and beauty and mystery of the sea. It is such a deeply moving religious experience. The sea is so vast and powerful and our ship, like our lives, is so small. We are so interdependent on the men of this ship, our families, countless others whose names we don't know or faces we may never see and above all on You, the Lord and Giver of Life. Give to us now an awareness of your presence. Keep those who have the watch alert this night and to the rest of the PARSONS crew give restful sleep, peace and the creative freshness of tomorrow's dawn. Amen.

1977, 15 February USS PARSONS (DDG 33).

Eternal God we marvel at the courage and stamina of men who do their job well in difficult situations. Our lives are generally so comfortable and secure. We have to endure hardship only rarely and then for only short periods of time. Make us aware of those persons whose daily lot forces them to endure the bitterness of cold or the gnawing emptiness of hunger without adequate clothes or food or shelter. We have so much while so many people in the world have so little. We pray this night for the orphans of Korea, Japan, Taiwan, and the Philippines. We are grateful for the kindness and generosity of American sailors who give that others may live. Jesus has made us aware that from those who have much, much is required. May it be said of us as it was of him, he did all things well. Make us discontent with less than our best. Amen.

1977, 16 February USS PARSONS (DDG 33).

Eternal God, today we watched with amazement the strange phenomenon of mist-like clouds low lying over the swells of the sea. We also felt tempestuous tossing as the ship rolled and pitched. We received warm and friendly greetings from men we know and came to know some persons we had not known before. Keep us ever open to the wonder of new experiences whether on the ever-changing sea or in revealing human relationships. Life is your great gift to be shared, so free us from fears that inhibit the joys of knowing others and being known by them. Give us lives that praise You for the privilege of being co-creators with You of our destinies. Strengthen us by your Spirit that we may live responsibly with one another, now and always. Amen.

1977, 17 February USS PARSONS (DDG 33).

O God, by what name shall we call You; in what places shall we look for You; at what times will we find You. For You have been known by so many names and been met in such different ways in strange places and unexpected times. Is it so strange that some men find it hard to acknowledge You? It is a miracle that we even accept and understand one another. We come from such different backgrounds, have had such varied experiences; we hold to such a variety of values. What do we have in common? At least that we are together on this ship safe in this harbor of Beppu. We share our humanity too. Long ago someone said that You have made us for yourself and we are restless until we rest in You. [St. Augustine]

O God, be our guide, our strength, our help as we seek a meaning big enough for us, a purpose satisfying to us, a commitment sufficient for our highest dreams and a fulfillment that knows no end now or ever. Amen.

1977, 15 July USS BAUSELL (DD845) at sea, no port visit.

It is good to be back aboard USS BAUSELL. If I have a ship's home this is it. You certainly make me feel I belong as one of you. There are many new men since I was last with you. Today I met several of them. They are fortunate sailors. May they learn from you not only the skills to find satisfaction in their work but the satisfaction of life well lived. Join me now in the Evening Prayer.

Eternal God, it has been a good day. The seas have been delightfully calm; the skies bright and clear. Old friendships have been renewed and new ones begun. In what better way do we become aware of your presence than through other people? Give us a strong sense of who we are, an appreciation of who we have become because of the influence of others, and an expectation of a richer and more complete life because of the confidence others have in us.

Bless the men of the BAUSELL and those they love and who love them. Make those who keep the watches of the night alert and to all others give rest and peace and renewal of life through restful sleep. Amen.

1977, 16 July USS BAUSELL (DD845).

My Lord what a day! What experiences we have shared! Some of us are lonely and afraid and far away from the familiar and comfortable. Some of us are covering up and trying to hide from others what we know about ourselves. Some of us are unsure of ourselves and insecure in our relationships with others. Come to us in our needs. Free us from fears by faith, from loneliness by friendship, from deception by acceptance, from insecurity by confidence.

May the one who did all things well, even Jesus Christ, our Lord, enable us to live affirmatively as sons of God. Amen.

1977, 17 July USS BAUSELL (DD845).

God, our Father, words are such powerful things. We hear the same words but they don't mean the same things to all of us. Our experiences are so varied, so diverse. Some of us have been given many advantages while others of us have been less fortunate. It is so easy for some to live life with confidence, control, and mastery that they sometimes lose patience with others who are less disciplined, less accomplished, or less determined. Give us patience with others as we expect from them the best of which they are capable. Let us not be satisfied with anything less than our best. We are grateful for every experience of this day which has brought encouragement, hope, and renewal for us. Give us now a peaceful night and the expectation of an even better tomorrow. In the spirit of the Christ, we pray. Amen.

1977, 18 July USS BAUSELL (DD845).

God it has been another beautiful day. We are grateful for smooth seas and clear skies and pleasant friendships. We are proud of the men of the BAUSELL - - of their ability to work well together and perform admirably. We realize how dependent we are on one another. Let us never take that for granted or lose our perspective or our sense of humor. It is good to be able to laugh with one another rather than at one another, to work with each other rather than against one another. Bring now the peace of your presence and a sense of well-being which comes from work well done.

To those whose day continues through the night bring strength sufficient for their needs and to all others give minds and hearts at ease to welcome and enjoy sleep and needed rest. Amen

1977, 19 July USS BAUSELL (DD845).

Eternal God, once again we offer our evening prayer. What can we say *that we haven't said before? What can we offer that isn't either too shallow or too remote to be of any value? Help us to be realistic and honest. Did we help make other men's live better or worse today? Were we careless or callous or unkind? Did we pretend it didn't matter to us what other people said or did to us or what we said or how we treated them? Did we forget that other men want what we want -- acceptance, understanding, honesty, worth, dignity, respect? Did we ignore someone else's need for privacy, for peace? Did we degrade them and ourselves by making fun of them?*

Don't get us wrong, O God, we're not asking to be perfect, or heroes, or saints. We simply want to say at the end of the day, "it was a good day"; to be able to say, "it's my life and I like it." Thanks for the awesome freedom to be responsible for our own lives. Give us this night peace and power to live as your sons. Amen.

1977, 20 July USS BAUSELL (DD845).

Eternal God, grand prayers seem to belong to grand occasions. But, life isn't always grand. In fact, so much of it is commonplace, and ordinary and every day.

It has been another beautiful day of sailing calm seas without excitement or spectacle. We are so prone to look for you in the strange and exotic architecture of cathedrals or temples, pagodas or pavilions that we sometimes neglect the reality of the divine presence of weather-decks or engine rooms, or shops and shacks, of bridges and berthing. We are glad that even when we are unaware of your presence You sustain us and support our lives. Bring us to an ever more satisfying life that comes from a deep gratitude not reserved for once-in-a-lifetime events. Open our eyes to the wonders of every day's gifts that we may close them with every night's thankfulness. Amen.

1977, 21 July USS BAUSELL (DD845).

O Lord, our God, You have given us life. We come from You and ultimately return to You. When we grow tired You strengthen us. When we become confused You help us straighten things out. When we sorrow You comfort us. When we disappoint ourselves You forgive us. When our spiritual resources run low You replenish us underway. You steady us in rough seas and give us joy in cruising calm and beautiful seas.

Let each time at sea be a religious renewal for us. Watch over those we love far away and whose love makes our life that much more worth living. We give

You thanks in everything, our Lord and our God. Amen.

1977, 16 August   USS KNOX (FF 1052) en-route   from   Pearl   Harbor,   Hawaii   to Yokosuka, Japan.

Eternal God, this night we are especially grateful for the calm seas of our transit and for the opportunity to get to know the men of the KNOX. We ask your particular blessing upon them as they reach their new home in Japan. Give to her Captain and officers a continued dedication tempered by wisdom and good humor, and to her crew a sense of admiration, respect and pride in being an able and ready ship. Open us to every expression of the divine that comes to us now in strange new ways. Fill us always with your love and the peace of your presence. Amen.

1977, 26 October aboard USS BAUSELL (DD 845) as she departed from Yokosuka, Japan for San Diego and decommissioning. The Commanding Officer,   Commander   John   H.   McMillan, requested   and   to   many   persons'   surprise received   approval   of   a   fantastic,   once-in-a-lifetime transit from Yokosuka to San Diego via Keelung,   Subic   Bay,   Hong   Kong,   Bangkok, Singapore,   Fiji,   Samoa,   Sydney,   Auckland,   and Pearl Harbor.

Eternal   God,   the   months   of preparation, the weeks of anticipation, and the days of expectation have come to fruition as the BAUSELL begins her memorable odyssey. For some it is a time of separation from those they love, for some it is a time of eagerness to be again with those they love, for all it is a time of exotic places and rare experiences. There is something sacred about setting out to sea. May whatever wrongs we have done, whatever hurts we have caused, whatever callousness or carelessness has made life more difficult for others than it ought to be find its response in the immensity of your love as vast and powerful and beautiful as the sea.

When this journey is ended may we be better men than when we began. Give us rest and peace, joy in living, and gladness in who we are. Amen.

1977, 27 October USS BAUSELL (DD 845) en-route from Yokosuka, Japan to Keelung, Taiwan.

Eternal God, we are grateful that we have eyes to see and spirits alive enough to enjoy the delights of sunset and moonlight. At times we are like children holding so tightly to the old and the familiar that we can't reach out to take and enjoy the new. At other times, again like children, our passion for the new lets us toss the familiar too casually away. Give us a sense of proportion in life -- a feel for the appropriate. Sharpen our ability to take life seriously but not so seriously as to miss the humor in our own inconsistencies and the improprieties of others. Teach us the profundity of simplicity -- the depth of the ordinary, the joy of human companionship, the cherished value of human conversation, the lasting happiness of shared life. Amen.

1977, 28 October USS BAUSELL (DD 845).

Eternal God, what inexpressible joy you have given us through the men of the USS BAUSELL. They are a special company of men. They are not gods but they have helped us to appreciate how good it is to be men. They are not perfect but they have repeatedly shown us that every man has the capacity to admire and appreciate goodness even when it eludes his grasp. They have unashamedly shared with us their hopes and dreams, their fears and loves, their sense of wonder at the starry heavens above or the mysteriously sacred sea around us. May they always go with You in calmness and peace even amidst the turbulence that reveals us to ourselves. May they be alert to every expression of your grandeur and responsive to every opportunity for human kindness. May *their strength be ever equal to the challenges that confront them and their satisfaction as lasting as your presence. May the BAUSELL wherever she sails be aware that your love is her destiny. Amen.*

1978, 15 January USS PARSONS (DDG 33) returning from Keelung, Taiwan to Yokosuka, Japan.

My last prayer at Sea while attached to DESRON FIFTEEN was aboard the PARSONS, It is ironic that my first prayer with the SQUADRON was aboard the same ship. Regrettably, that prayer cannot be located.

C. Prayers on Other Occasions

1. Change of Command Ceremonies

1976, 30 July Yokosuka, Japan aboard USS LOCKWOOD (FF 1064), Captain Lawrence Penny relieved by Commander Gerald G. Stevens.

Eternal Father, for as long as men have put out to sea they have felt the mysterious and awesome power of your presence with them. For as long as men have joined together in sailing ships they have been dependent on each other and known success by their sense of pride in belonging to one another. Traditions and rituals have made the tedium and struggles somehow more bearable. In this Change of Command Ceremony, an honored tradition of the sea, we acknowledge our gratitude to you for the leadership of the Commanding Officer of USS LOCKWOOD. Grant to Captain Penny a sense of satisfaction in the accomplishment of his mission, anticipation and high expectation for his new responsibilities, and quiet confidence as he leaves this command. To the new Commanding Officer, Commander Stevens, grant renewed resources of devotion hot only to his mission for our Nation's Navy and the peace of mankind, but to dedicated leadership and human concern for those by whose respect and faithfulness his success is so largely measured. We praise You for your constant care and are grateful for your all-sufficient strength. Amen.

1976, 16 August Yokosuka, Japan aboard USS PARSONS (DDG 33), Captain Gerald A. Fulk relieved by Commander Walter T. Dziedzic, Jr.

Eternal Father, we come now to a time of celebration and ceremony as men have done for as long as they have set out together to sail the mysterious seas. We are aware that it is a naval ritual noble in intent and honorable in execution. We are also aware that it is a *religious ceremony awesome in responsibility and beneficent in commendation. Something deep within us calls forth our integrity in the highest uses of the intelligence, sensitivity, and leadership with which we have been endowed. In this Change of Command Ceremony we pray thy blessing on Captain Fulk as he leaves the command of USS PARSONS to assume new and challenging responsibilities in his naval career. Grant to him continued tranquility, satisfaction, and fulfillment as he reflects on his accomplishments here. Grant to Commander Dziedzic committed dedication which balances mission readiness with the fullest human development possible of those who look to him for direction and purpose. On this significant occasion, rekindle in the officers and men of this ship pride in being members of the United States Navy in pursuit of peace, international and intercultural appreciation and acceptance, and broader human community. Amen.*

1976, 01 October Yokosuka, Japan pier-side Captain Clifford L. Bekkedahl relieved by Captain Joel H. Berry, Jr. as Commodore of Destroyer Squadron Fifteen (CDS 15). I am unable to locate these Invocation and Benediction prayers.

2. Chaplain's Notes

Often when riding a ship the Chaplain is invited to write a "Chaplain's Note" to be included in the Plan of the Day which contains the Captain's Orders for the day, the daily schedule and other pertinent information including when and where daily Bible Study would be held.

I regret that I can find only a couple of these but print them here as examples of another way a Chaplain is able to encourage sacred moments.

1977, 17 July USS BAUSELL (DD 845).

We all need time to sort things out to see where we're going. People often say, "I'm all mixed up, confused, messed up; I don't know what's going on or what to do." Sometimes they want a fast, magical answer from religion. But religion isn't magic - it doesn't make the problems go away. It can, however, give a sense of projection, perspective, and balance. It can help you realize that you are not alone and that there are always divine resources for dealing with our problems, failures, or disappointments. Worship with me this morning at 0900 on the flight deck - it may make a real difference in your life.

1977, 20 July USS BAUSELL (DD 845)

There are a lot of homely sayings that go a long way to coping with situations. For instance, "you have to go from where you are," helps accept the reality of the present and avoid the wistful remembering of things as they were, which they usually weren't anyway. Or, "where you stand determines what you see," does a lot to realize we don't come at life, or live it, in the same way. Or, "there's only one life I can really do anything about, and that's my own," can sure cut down on fretting over someone else's weaknesses.

What you believe about life really makes a difference: a little optimism, a little caution, a lot of trust, a lot of confidence, some determination, some enthusiasm, a firm commitment to give back more to life than you take from it are more realistic than defeatism, cynicism, pessimism, and a general, "I don't give a damn" approach.

Fortunately, there is a whole lot of the former and very little of the latter on the BAUSELL. I don't know your secret, but I surely do admire it.

Chapter II.
USS PELELIU (LHA 5),
Long Beach, California,
February, 1980-August, 1982.

A. The privilege of serving as a plank owner on a newly commissioned ship.

To be a plank owner of a newly constructed vessel is an honor which few in the Navy get to experience.

After my tour with COMDESRON FIFTEEN (CDS 15) I served the men and women of FIRST SERVICE SUPPORT GROUP (1st FSSG), USMC, Camp Pendleton, These assignments prepared me well for serving as Chaplain on an amphibious ship responsible for transporting and supporting Marines.

I received orders to report to San Diego to become part of the crew of the ship to be commissioned USS PELELIU (LHA 5).

I checked in with Commander Paul Guay, the Prospective Executive Officer who was in charge of the San Diego contingent overseeing training and molding us into a crew fit for the opportunities that would be ours to serve on what some were calling "the Cadillac of the fleet." Each of us went through fire-fighting school and damage control training to prepare us to work as a team.

It was a pleasure to work with the XO throughout most of my tour and then with his successor Commander J.H. Bower, Jr. both of whom were selected for Captain as rightly they should have been.

After a few weeks we were visited by Captain Thomas P. Scott, our Prospective Commanding Officer who was leading the other half of the crew in Pascagoula.

Captain Scott was an unassuming man with a great sense of humor and the rare ability to take his work seriously while not letting that cause him to take himself too seriously. He had flown A 7s in Vietnam and Commanded USS CORONADO (LPD 11) before being selected as the man to lead this remarkable amphibious ship nearing completion of construction at Ingall's Shipyard in Pascagoula, Mississippi.

He called me Chaps and I called him Cap'n; we still do after all these years.

We sat in two overstuffed chairs in a room by ourselves beginning one of the finest friendships I could ever want. He talked unpretentiously about his hopes and expectations for the ship and what he expected of his Chaplain. He reduced it to a couple of things: Take care of the Crew and their families and Make sure there would be sunshine on the day of commissioning. I tried my best to fulfill those directives.

The Commissioning was weeks away and when we had finished our training in San Diego we all joined the Pascagoula contingent. A couple of days before the Commissioning Ceremony was to take place the CO sent me a Memo he had received from the meteorologist: 24 Hour Outlook: Continued mostly cloudy skies through Sunday with scattered rain and thunder showers through Saturday morning. Good chance that the shower activity will continue through Saturday evening. The Cap'n had highlighted in red the message and written in his inimitable red pen "Maybe it's time to call in the 'Big Guns'! (Chaplain)."

The night before the Commissioning, there was a gala celebration on the lawn of a palatial old Southern mansion. However, we were soon driven inside by heavy rain squalls.

The next morning, the day of Commissioning, the rain poured bountifully upon us as we began to gather pier-side for the ceremony. About one hour before the commencement of the festivities the wind ceased, the clouds moved away and the sun broke brightly through. Thanks be to God!

On Friday afternoon we had a dress rehearsal complete with loose-leaf binder for each person's part including the invocation and benediction by the Chaplain. As the Ceremony began I went to the podium and opened the binder to the page for the invocation. There was no invocation. Instead someone had inserted a full-page centerfold from *Playboy*. As I invited the assembled crowd to pray with me I removed my cover (that's Navy language for hat) and looked down at a copy of the prayer which I had stowed away there. All went well from there and Mrs. Peggy Hayward, the Ship's Sponsor and wife of Admiral Thomas B. Hayward, Chief of Naval Operations   proudly acknowledged the commissioning of this grand lady of the sea USS PELELIU (LHA 5) which she had christened on 06 January 1979.

The Commanding Officer of a ship chooses a "break-way" song used when the ship leaves pier or breaks away from replenishment at sea. Captain Scott chose Willie Nelson's "On the Road Again". It still resonates with me after all these years and memories of that first casting off from Pascagoula putting us on the road again, or sea as it were.

One of the first things Captain Scott had done for his unknown Chaplain was designating the stateroom adjacent to his in-port cabin as the Chaplain's Stateroom. It was fortuitous for that allowed us to spend many a pleasant evening sharing our knowledge and experiences and mutual concerns for the Ship and its crew.

He and I spent a good bit of time roaming the Ship together speaking to each man as we went. We made a good team – he knew every man's last name and I knew each man by his first name. Because it was a new ship there was stability in the crew for several months enabling it to become a commendable naval unit.

While in Pascagoula, the wardroom bonded with many evenings spent along the bayou listing to Linda Ronstadt singing "Blue Bayou", recorded, of course. The crew too found cohesion and in a remarkable way we all became part of one anothers lives from the beginning believing our destinies were inseparable.

Just recalling these experiences brings back memories and images of an exceptional group of men. I feel remiss in not mentioning them all by name. However, I hope those not mentioned will not hold it against me and will know how deeply I appreciate their unique contributions.

One of the senior enlisted made an indelible impression each Monday morning when new men reporting aboard attended Orientation. The Captain welcomed them and set the bar high by his expectations. The Executive Officer shared some practical advice often with a touch of humor. The Chaplain encouraged them to make the most of the remarkable opportunity that was now theirs as PELELIU crewmen. The climax however, was when Master Chief Tom Wallace, Chief Master at Arms, stood as if he had a board down his back, thrusting his chest full of ribbons forward, planting his right foot in front of him, directing his index finger at each of them and in a voice they would never forget proclaimed, "Remember men there is no second chance for a first impression."

From the Captain down everyone expected the best of himself and others. Sometimes that just didn't happen. Not long after we left Pascagoula I went at the appointed time to the Bridge to give the Evening Prayer. It was a pitch-black night and the men on Bridge watch had adjusted their eyes for night-vision.

I gave the Prayer and tried to slip unobtrusively off the Bridge. When I reached for the release to the door I inadvertently hit the light switch and it was as if a million watts were illuminating the place. After a few appropriate curses from some of the Watch Standers I slipped unceremoniously away. The next morning I expected to receive at least a mild dressing down from the Captain. Instead he said, "I had the HTs go up this morning and put a guard over that switch so it can't happen again."

That was the true spirit of the man. I attended almost every Captain's Mast he held and invariably found him to be fair, just and humane and often merciful as he had been with me when I made the night into day.

Several times when we were in port Long Beach, our homeport, the Ship's bus would take about 25 or 30 men for a day's work stringing barbed wire or planting trees at Children's Village near Beaumont, CA, some distance away. The PELELIU received recognition from celebrities at a luncheon at Century Plaza Hotel. This was one of several awards the PELELIU would receive for her humanitarian service. I had left my cover (cap) on the hat rack outside the ballroom. When I came out someone had taken it as a souvenir.

Whenever we were in foreign ports large numbers of officers and enlisted visited orphanages doing physical work like painting and repairing buildings, digging gardens or uprooting encroaching bamboo, and delivering humanitarian supplies and playing with the children. These Project Handclasp endeavors in Thailand, the Philippines, Australia and elsewhere were enthusiastic expressions of the generosity and kindness of PELELIU Sailors.

Hospitality is an apt word to apply to the PELELIU. She was superb at it whether on the receiving end, as at SEAFAIR in Seattle or the giving end in port Long Beach.

In foreign ports she often received dignitaries including heads of state; at home a vast array of high ranking Navy and Marine Corps Officers were received with proper ceremonial attention by the Captain and crew. On one occasion Captain Scott and a full complement of side-boys waited for one hour for the arrival of a Chief of Chaplains. The Captain had everyone standby and when the honored guest arrived he was received as courteously as if he had arrived at the appointed time.

Captain Scott and the XO took time from their busy schedules not just to make a ceremonial welcome but to sit and talk and listen to our guests.

Several of the crewmen brought their church groups and choirs. The Chaplain hosted ministers of his denomination (Christian Church, Disciples of Christ) from Southern California led by one of his former students at Transylvania. Other times Naval Reserve Chaplains from Southern California came for training as a group and spent the better part of a morning conversing with the CO and XO. When the Chaplain's denomination held its General Assembly in nearby Anaheim tours of the PELELIU were conducted and were well attended; again hosted by the CO.

A very special expression of hospitality by the CO and crew was a visit by my endorsing agent, Chaplain Robert Tindall, Colonel, US Air Force (Retired) and his remarkable wife Mildred. Bob had guided me through the endorsing process and visited me annually wherever I was stationed. Now he was retiring. The Captain graciously hosted a splendid retirement dinner, with appropriate gifts, for them at the Officers Club, Naval Station, Long Beach. I had never seen Bob happier and more gratified. I could not have been prouder to be Chaplain of the PELELIU.

There are so many experiences which are worth sharing but I must limit them to a few which give more of a context for the prayers.

We were an amphibious ship built to transport Marines and off-load them by boat and helicopter; we were also a launching platform for Marine VSTOLS/Harriers. Their take offs and landings were quite a sight as they hovered like hummingbirds setting down on the flight deck. In addition we were configured to expand the medical facilities into a three hundred bed hospital if the need should arise for humanitarian evacuation of American personnel from hostile conditions in foreign countries.

We drilled and practiced, practiced and drilled perfecting the arts and skills needed to fulfill with excellence any mission we might be assigned.

We transported Marines and often had their Chaplains embarked. From time to time the Amphibious Squadron Staff was embarked and their Chaplain became a part of life aboard. Since I was a Protestant and our incredible Captain was a devout Roman Catholic I took every opportunity to avail ourselves of the ministries of Roman Catholic Chaplains. Several enriched our lives but none more generously than Father Brian Kane who was stationed at Naval Station, Long Beach who found it possible to ride us from time to time. Father Kane indelibly became part of the PELELIU family participating in our Christmas parties and other social events. It was hard to believe he was not a full-fledged member of the PELELIU crew.

Our humanitarian training was put to the test when we came across a dilapidated boat off Vietnam filled with old men, women and children. After they were brought aboard the PELELIU their unseaworthy craft was soon at the bottom of the sea. They were well cared for by the medical staff and others who took a personal interest in their welfare. Some of our senior enlisted men were fluent in Vietnamese and made their frightened transition easier. Senior Chief Long who led a weekly Sunday School class on WESTPAC and was recipient of the Claude V. Ricketts Award for Inspirational

Leadership was as compassionate and fluent an ambassador as we could have wanted.

We disembarked the much improved Refugees in Thailand turning them over to the American Embassy which arranged for their transfer to the United Nations High Commissioner's Camp for Refugees in the Philippines.

It was our good fortune to see them later adjusting to their new life and preparing for their future in America or Europe.

One of the most glorious Easters I have ever known was in Pearl Harbor when the Pacific Fleet Chaplain conducted Mass on the flight deck with a significant number of officers and men in attendance. Captain Scott was in the front row as always and our very capable young Eucharistic Lay Leader, Lieutenant, JG Jim McCabe assisted the Chaplain in the service.

The finest Religious Program Specialist I ever worked with, RP2 Mark Goffrier, had procured dozens of Easter lilies from a local florist and had set up everything to the glory of God and the satisfaction of our visiting Chaplain/Priest. I was truly fortunate to be supported in ministry by such dedicated RPs as Mark and RP2 Mike Borens among others.

One of the things a sea-going Chaplain learns is that though his service is to each and all men and women that does not translate into great crowds for worship services. More often than not only a handful of the crew showed up for Morning Worship whether at sea or ashore.

So much of a Chaplain's ministry is one to one. The Chaplain's Office was located just off the enlisted mess deck and near the Post Office. This meant there was not a day went by that several men stopped by for a visit. Some were just friendly chats others pushed us to the depths of compassion and concern.

Almost every Monday morning for several months when we first arrived in Long Beach one young sailor stopped by to tell me he had spent the week-end looking for his father whom he had never seen since he left the family right after the young man was born. I would ask how the search went and he would cheerfully reply, "I haven't found him yet Chaplain but I'm getting closer." Then one morning the mood was entirely different. I could read it on his face but he needed to tell me. "I went up to the door where I knew he lived and he answered it, looked at me and said, 'get out of here; I never want to see you. As far as I'm concerned you don't exist." There were far too many Sailors in the various commands I served who said they could not remember a single time when their Dad had put his arm around them or hugged them or said simply "I'm proud of you" or "I love you." What a terrible burden to carry through life.

One Sunday morning I had finished the morning worship in the little chapel/library and was ready to depart the ship when the Command Duty Officer stopped me and informed me that one of our Sailors had been run over by a city bus and killed instantly in the middle of the night. He was in the Los Angeles morgue and the Coroner needed positive identification. The Officer of the Deck and I drove to the morgue and performed one of the most heart-wrenching duties any one has to perform. The Ship took his death to heart and joined in a meaningful Memorial Service when we put out to sea again.

It was not all sadness and sorrow. On the PELELIU we were blessed with senior Non-Commissioned Petty Officers and Chiefs who led regular Bible studies and worship services for their particular faith group as is noted in some of the prayers. There were weddings and christenings and anniversaries and reenlistments and birthdays a plenty. What joy!

I could not have been an effective chaplain had it not been first of all for the unstinting encouragement and support of the Commanding and Executive Officers and every Department Head, especially the Supply Department Head Commander Ken Casanova and his very able assistant LCDR Jim Holcomb for working on pay and support issues for crewmembers and the Administrative Department Head Lieutenant Rich James to whom I turned daily for personnel matters. I am still deeply grateful to all the wonderful team members.

B. Evening Prayers at Sea

These prayers were offered aboard USS PELELIU (LHA 5) from 13 May 1980, the first night at sea after commissioning at Pascagoula, Mississippi 03 May 1980 until my detachment 02 August, 1982 at Subic Bay, the Philippines. Other Chaplains, when embarked, offered evening prayers over the 1 MC, but those are not included here.

My entire tour was served with Captain Thomas P. Scott, USN, Commanding Officer. The prayers not only give some indication of our love for God and His people but provide a spiritual log of the more significant events in the life of the ship and her crew. These Sacred Moments were offered to God and listened to by the men to an exceptionally gratifying extent.

1980, 13 May. First night at sea in the Gulf of Mexico en-route from Pascagoula, Mississippi to homeport Long Beach, California.

This is Chaplain Murphey. Evening Prayers are a time honored tradition of our Navy. So each evening between tattoo and taps we will pause to offer our prayer to God.

Eternal God, it happened so smoothly, so beautifully, so well -- that very first day at sea for so many among us. The days of preparation, the weeks and even months of long hours and tedious labor by so many are now somehow well worth it. Some among us will work while others sleep as we make our way across the silent sea. Bless those who stand watch this night as well as those who sleep that both may have a sense of satisfaction and pride at being a vital part of this magnificent ship and its marvelous crew. You have blessed us richly, bless us still by a grateful awareness of your creative power and love. Amen.

1980, 14 May.

At the close of this day which has brought to some the incredible joy of the beauty of the sea in religious appreciation too deep for words, we pause for our evening prayer.

Father God, we have heard it said, "many are called but few are chosen," and it has new meaning, new depth for us the chosen ones who man this great ship. We thank You that almost without exception each man sets about his tasks with the earnest conviction that the quality of his service is a gift he offers You joyously from his own integrity, for his own satisfaction and for the well-being of all those who depend on his labor. To some You have given much and from them much is required. We pray this night a special prayer for our Commanding Officer to whom has been given the awesome responsibility and rare privilege of command. You have equipped him well for so formidable a task. We thank you for the challenge and grace of his leadership which demanding so much from so many inspires what it commands - their very best. To all of us give now, we pray, the peace of your presence whether in well-earned sleep or dutiful watch. Amen.

1980, 15 May.

Eternal God, it is so amazing how some days seem so right and other days just have a vague uneasiness about them. The sky was clear enough and the sea was as beautifully blue as we could appreciate or enjoy. But there was a kind of strain, a tension, a pulling in too many directions. It makes us all the more aware how very difficult wholeness, integrity, unity is to achieve and sustain whether in our own lives as persons or in that combined life we share as ship's company. Our lives depend on so many *others for whom we offer prayerful thanks.*

We offer a special prayer tonight for our Executive Officer. He must combine the sometimes thankless task of coordinating and orchestrating and of keeping myriad objectives, programs and approaches on track and on time. We are grateful for his good humor, his openness and honesty about himself, and his fairness and humane concern for others. Give him a special grace to enjoy the creative amidst the overwhelmingly ordinary necessities. And to all of us this night grant a renewed spirit, a belief that you working in us and through us can keep it all together in both our personal and our interpersonal lives in a most satisfying way. Amen.

1980, 16 May approaching the Panama Canal.

Eternal God, we offer to You once again our heartfelt thanks for gifts so small that their very presence makes them great. The friendly greeting, the smile, the word of good cheer, the shared wonder of the immensity of the calm sea or the awesome pleasantness of that moment between the day's bright heat and the evening's cool reassurance. We wonder at it all and marvel at the vastness and ask again with the poet of long ago, "When I consider the vastness of the heavens what is a man that you even care for him?" We receive our answer as clearly now as it has ever been, "You have created us like yourself, a little less than gods."

Help us Lord to honor that gift, that great love. And with the trust of obedient sons who place themselves ever anew in our Father's care and keeping let us with each night's rest and each day's work accept the impress of your eternal spirit upon our human lives. Amen.

1980, 26 May   in the Pacific Ocean after transiting the Panama Canal and liberty in Panama City.

As we are underway again we resume our evening prayers. Would you pause with me on this Memorial Day for the evening prayer?

God of our Fathers and our God, we are mindful this night that our life as a nation is a life passed on to us at great cost. Our fathers had a dream that men and women of all sorts and kinds, of varied races and colors, of deep religious commitment or little religious devotion, of substantial wealth or struggling for survival could somehow live together as a free and democratic people. While they desired peace they sometimes found themselves engaged in war.

We remember this night those who at the island of Peleliu in a time before *most of us were born did what they felt compelled to do and offered themselves a sacrifice that the dream would become a closer reality. Not all of the valiant died there. Some of them are among us and inspire us to our own honorable service in the cause of peace. We thank you that they have lived the conviction that when nations no longer must be enemies their peoples may become friends.*

We the men of USS PELELIU now gratefully offer our prayers to You for the sacrifices of those who died and those who lived at Peleliu. Amen.

1980, 27 May in the Pacific Ocean approaching the Equator.

As we offer our evening prayer to You, oh God, we ask your blessing on those who await our return. We have chosen the way of the sea and there is pride in being part of something grand and significant. We appreciate more clearly every day our dependence on one another and the privilege and responsibility of doing our work well for the sake of others.

There is the excitement of ceremonies and destinations, of liberty, bringing us new faces and places. For those at home there is the ordinary and often monotonous routine of caring for children and coping with the stresses and strains of too many bills and too little money. There are always tedious hours as they await our return. As we are confident that You are with us as we follow our dream, may we also be aware that they too are in your care and keeping. Bless, oh Lord, our wives and children and deepen our love for them and theirs for us.

We ask tonight a special prayer that the revelry of our crossing the line tomorrow may be unmarred by any action which would divide us. May what we do be a bond between us. Let the satisfaction of those who initiate be equaled by the welcomed relief and pride of those received into that closer relationship of men of the sea who share never-to-be-forgotten rites of passage. Amen.

1980, 28 May in the Pacific Ocean north of the Equator.

Benevolent God, we are glad that You have given to us a sense of humor, the ability to laugh at ourselves and with others. We thank You that we may sometimes take serious things playfully and at other times playful things seriously. We thank You tonight for the earnest efforts of the few who provided so memorable a ceremony of Crossing the Line and did it with such restraint and *respect for one another's humanity. The tiredness and soreness will soon be forgotten but the joyful memories will be with us to share with our children and our children's children.*

In our special prayers tonight we are particularly appreciative of the Supply Department. We are grateful that we have been blessed with so skillful and dedicated a group of men as Commander Casanova, his officers, chiefs, petty officers and seamen who feed, cloth, and pay us and provide the materials so essential to our jobs. Without their efficiency and persistence we could not operate effectively or happily. In their never ending labors give them always strength and patience and the good grace to serve others in a spirit of kindliness.

And to each of us now grant a night of peaceful rest or wakeful watch. Amen.

1980, 29 May.

Before the prayer let me say in praying special prayers we are very much aware how important each man on this ship is. As we lift certain members up in prayer we are reminded of countless others. So I hope with each night's prayer you are encouraged to remember others in your private prayers. Now let us pray.

Gracious God, tonight we pray for the men who fly and for all those who support them in flight. They are a colorful and at times flamboyant lot. They are genial and affably social as well as resolute and authoritative in the performance of their duties. Because theirs is a life poised precariously on the illusive edge of danger a bit more frequently than some of ours, we ask that you continually give them steady nerves and mental agility in the dynamic interplay of control and release. So much time is spent by some in waiting, prepared in hot suits or flight deck gear for awful events they hope will never occur. Keep them ever vigilant.

For Commander Schiller, our Air Boss and his valiant men we are grateful. Such heavy responsibilities for so many lives are theirs. Their professionalism commands our admiration. For Lieutenant Commander Campbell and his able complement of specialists, resourceful and persistent, we are grateful. We pray also with gratitude for Major Gross and the Marine pilots and crewmembers of the helicopters. May their courage and daring be equaled by their lasting trust in one another and in You.

Bless now each PELELIU sailor and all those embarked with whatever gift of *peace or faith, empathy or hope, understanding or acceptance he might need to live a full and satisfying life. Amen.*

1980, 30 May.

God we are thankful that You have given to man the struggle to create, to fabricate, to fashion and that we live in an age when the technological skills of man's creative genius test and try us. As our machinery has become more and more complicated it has caused us to become more highly skilled, better educated, and quicker in our responses to crises and casualties. We hear often enough of the problems of our Navy from the demand for higher and higher levels of technical competence. So we are grateful this night for the strength and competence of our engineers.

We marvel at the almost inconceivable mass of knowledge of men and machines required of our Chief Engineer, Commander Rhodes and those who depend upon and are responsive to his leadership. To his officers and chiefs, his petty officers and firemen fall the stupendous task of running powerful boilers and engines which propel us toward our assigned destinations upon demand. What an intricate maze of electrical generation and circuitry they must supply and maintain. What a phenomenal mass of machinery they repair and keep on line. These men -- boiler techs and machinery repairmen, hull technicians and internal communicationists -- provide for our sanitation as well as our comfort and communication with one another. On them we rely for the integrity and damage control of our ship. Many of them spend arduous hours in the bowels of the ship with valves and pumps amidst heat and noise most of us are not subjected to.

They are a hardy group. They work hard and play hard. Protect them from carelessness or loss of confidence. Give to them a special measure of strength to match their fatiguing labors and lack of sleep. Theirs is a very tangible satisfaction when all goes well and an equally obvious dissatisfaction when it doesn't. So bless them and all of us through them now and always. Amen.

1980, 31 May.

God of the earth, the skies, the seas as we continue our voyage bringing us closer to those we love and the anticipation mounts for many of a liberty port, we become conscious of the intricate details of planning and operation, unfailing constancy of communication and precise calculation so essential to our safe and successful passage. So tonight we offer our prayer of gratitude to You for our Operations, Communications, and Navigation Departments. Their work is a frequent reminder that the life of a ship, even so fine a ship as this, is not self-sufficient. We are ever bound by the plans, regulations and will of higher command, dependent on the timely transmission and reception of messages through the atmosphere and upon the utilization of knowledge of currents and courses, depths and dangers.

We are truly grateful for Commander Reeves and all those who assist him in his multifaceted yet unified task. His poise and demeanor, his record of achievement on behalf of all colors and both sexes of naval personnel, and his pursuit of excellence breeds assurance and calm. To him and his people falls the responsibility for scheduling of movements, of training, of watch standing. Theirs is the responsibility of gathering, storing and retrieving data of weather and intelligence and making meaningful use of it. We delight in their making it possible through CCTV for us to be informed of a wide world beyond us as well as the world within the confines of our ship.

For Lieutenant Commander Grim, so ably intent on performing well his crucial task and his dedicated coterie of radiomen and signalmen who must exploit the process of transmission and reception we are most appreciative. What a range of concerns flow back and forth through them of technical information as well as the sometimes sorrowful, sometimes joyous contacts with those dependent on us and on whom we depend. Bless them in the tedious watches where one mistaken cipher could hold tragic consequences that their stamina of mind and body may be ever equal to their guard.

For Lieutenant Commander Barber and his quartermasters we offer our sincere thanks. His is a knowledge derived from a love of the sea and a demonstrated heroism against its violent power. Because he knows so much of the dangers of the deep there is a profound respect for charts and compasses and those who with him must plot our course with accuracy and speed.

What a wonderful company of shipmates you have blessed us with, oh God. Look upon us all with favor this night and tomorrow in our recreations and re-creation. Amen.

1980, 1 June.

Eternal God, we thank you for this Sunday. It was good to share the encouragement of Christian worship as well as the enthusiastic recreation of our first holiday routine at sea.

We are grateful again for the labors of our engineers who seem to be called upon often for an extra measure of service.

Tonight we offer a special prayer for our Deck and Combat Systems Departments and for the Combat Cargo Detachment.

Lieutenant Commander Mayo bestrides the deck an imposing presence dedicated to the mastery of a work as old as naval history. He, his boats'n mates, and seamen are in the longest line of descent of seafaring people. In the earliest days theirs was the backbreaking chore of pulling oars and wrestling tillers. They were hoisters and trimmers of sails unprotected by the ship's skin against driving winds and tumultuous waves that threatened to wash them away without a trace. Theirs has always been the muscle, determined will and forceful voice. They are the line handlers, boatsmen, steerers and exterior maintainers. It is as if the legends of the sea were written on their faces, if not tattooed on their arms. We thank you for these mighty sailors.

To Lieutenant Commander Mohn and his combat systems technicians falls a task so highly sophisticated it would have been inconceivable to their grandfathers. It is not enough that they must handle and stow ammunition with nerves of steel; they must also keep armament and ordnance ever ready. As they work with electronic weaponry and fire control systems so finely tuned that there is not the slightest room for error what pressures and tensions they must endure. Their data systems appear to the uninitiated as baffling as wizardry. Sustain them always in that calculated coolness so characteristic of them where restraint must not give way to too quick or too delayed an appropriate action or response.

We thank you, oh God, for Captain Faunce, Tops Frazier and Weber and Gunney Cooper. They are a select detachment of seagoing Marines. On their repetitive planning and rehearsing will largely depend the successful execution of amphibious operations for which our ship was designed and constructed. We thank you for these particular Marines who add much to our capabilities and camaraderie.

Father, we pray that should we be called upon to use our weaponry and amphibious assault capabilities we may be forgiven. We have long since realized that in the world in which we live we cannot afford the luxury of moral purity. Yet, men of moral commitment and integrity must acquit themselves honorably in tasks to which fainter spirits could never respond.

Grant us now peace within and keep alive always peace among us as each responds to tasks to which he was called or chosen. Amen.

1980, 2 June in the Pacific Ocean approaching Mazatlan, Mexico.

Dear God, tonight our circle of prayer for our shipmates completes itself as we offer You our gratitude for the Medical/Dental Department and the Executive Department.

We thank you for Doctors Guzley and Wheeler, Senior Chief Garman and our corpsmen and dental techs. What a fortunate blend of youthful exuberance, idealism, and brilliance with stabilizing compassionate care. We pray that they may not be called upon often to alleviate suffering but are confident that each such call will meet with devoted and expert response. They are men of noble integrity. They acquit themselves admirably in keeping our secrets when we have acquired excess baggage we dare not carry home and act with proper openness and urgency when illness or disease debilitates one of us. Bless them Lord for they indeed are a tremendous blessing to us.

While our whole ship is an unusually person-oriented ship reflecting the avowed commitment of our remarkable Captain, there is a small group that has the responsibility of being the right hands of the Captain and XO. No one better exemplifies devotion to duty in often prosaic and monotonously routine tasks than does Lieutenant James, our Ship's Secretary and Executive Department Head. As we offer our prayer of gratitude each individual in the department comes to mind. You know them all and we appreciate each one of them greatly. They provide our personnel services of record keeping and correspondence, educational and religious service, printing and postal services, legal matters and police function. Every one of us is dependent on them in innumerable ways. We would all drown in a sea of paper if they did not steer so accurate a course through these rocks and shoals. The ordinary task of maintaining good order and discipline, whether of records or crewmen, is staggering enough in itself but it is in response to special needs, such as emergency leave that they shine brightest. Accept our thanks for these our cherished shipmates.

One last word tonight, Our father. An awful lot of men did outstanding work today which says by its appearance I'm proud of my ship and glad to be here. To those who must keep the watches of the night in spite of their weariness give the support of your strength and to all others give now a well-earned and restful sleep and tomorrow a good and pleasant liberty. Amen.

1980, 7 June in the Pacific Ocean en-route to San Diego from Mazatlan, Mexico

Well God pardon the break in our conversation but as you know we were in port and the schedule is a bit different then. We're back at sea again and awfully glad to be heading home. These times of prayer mean a great deal to us and we pray they have meaning for You as well.

Help us to listen as well as to speak; to recognize your divine presence in things natural and human. Open us to the joys and sorrows of human life. How privileged we are to have new experiences, to run new risks, to share new joys in different places among people new to us. But help us in these neither to make too much or too little of our encounters. Help us to enjoy other people without guilt or shame.

You know us, God. Sailors are always looking for a relationship - we go after it in different ways - but we really want to be with someone and feel it matters to them and it all makes sense somehow. We want to believe that in the midst of all the confusion and put-downs and strain of living we are important. Help us in our seeking to realize that other people want that too, whether that other person is our shipmate, our wife, our children, our parents, or the girl we meet on the beach or in the bar. Help us to grow up into a kind of manhood which satisfies our restlessness even as it adds to other people's lives.

Give to each of us what each one needs for maturity and receive from us those expressions of ourselves offered to others which will allow them to pray, "Thanks God, I'm glad that he's around." Beyond all the phoniness and charades help us to love ourselves as you intend in such a way that we are then free to love You and other persons. Amen.

1980, 8 June.

God, our Father, what a good feeling it is to be a part of a ship that does all things well. What satisfaction there is for all of us in the attitude and spirit of the men with whom we work. We have known other ships where cancerous negativism gnaws away at morale, sapping the vitality of crew making men ashamed of themselves for having been placed there and often bitterly accusing their shipmates. We wish they could know the joy of men who have confidence in one another and in themselves, men convinced that they cannot fail because they are supported by so many, men who rejoice in the firm belief that one man succeeds only when there is success for all.

We offer a special prayer tonight for those men who have made the transit with us, men like Larry Schwartz from Long Beach, Troy Ziglar from the Navy League, Hal and John and Fred and all the others from Ingalls, Lee and all the other tech reps. Our lives are always enriched by people who have unique contributions or needed information or beneficial influence. We are particularly grateful for our Pace instructors who have worked patiently to expand the horizons of those of us who at real sacrifice have sought to deepen our knowledge and abilities.

We thank you for that rare individual Jack Fichter and all the others whose names we won't mention but who nonetheless have blessed us by becoming a part of our life together. When time comes for them to leave us may they go as ambassadors of goodwill on behalf of the PELELIU.

Now grant us that restfulness which comes from the satisfaction of a job well done and the inspiration and power to be able to say also ours is a life well lived. Amen.

1980, 9 June last night at sea before entering San Diego and after a brief stay sailing on to Long Beach, our home port.

Eternal God, we offer our prayer tonight with the anticipation and excitement of men who having shared the labors and learning of our first voyage together now look forward to the joys and comforts of home.

We have learned much about our ship -- some of her capabilities, her idiosyncrasies, her performance in different situations. We have learned more about one another -- some of our strengths and weaknesses, some of the points at which we are sensitive or vulnerable, some of our personal hurts or public pride. We know ourselves a bit better also. We know all too well that we are not gods, none of us. But, we know it is a great thing to be a man; even a man with fantasies, fears and failures.

Help us to accept one another without the necessity of making others over into likenesses of ourselves. Let us receive from others such acceptance as will set us free to strive after the best of which we are capable.

While our public prayers will not be shared for a while help us to continue our private conversation with You for You alone are our God, the Lord. from whom we have come. To You we will ultimately return.

We have been given the privilege of being co-creators with You of our destinies for which we bear the responsibility of gratitude and the accountability of fulfillment. As wise men before us have prayed, "Protect us all the day long of this troublous life until the day is spent and the evening shadows lengthen and the noise of life is hushed." [John Henry Cardinal Newman] Fill us with peace and bring us home safe at last. Amen.

1980, 7 July in the Pacific Ocean, SOCAL (Southern California Operating Area).

Eternal God there are several new shipmates who have joined us since we gave You thanks for this remarkable crew. Though we wish they could have been with us from the start we are glad they are now a part of us. Help us who shared the exciting birth of this ship to remember what it is like to be the new man -- the hesitancy, the uncertainty, the uneasiness. Let us make an extra effort to welcome them, to communicate our confidence in them, and encourage the very best they have to offer. We thank You for a gift equal to every man's uniqueness - the ability and desire to become a part of the finest crew of sailors in our Navy, to give their best and expect no less.

Keep our vision clear lest we perish in mediocrity. Keep our devotion firm lest we drown in our own failures. Keep faithful our awareness that You alone are our Lord and God, the source of our dreams, our hope, our destiny. Let us live in the quietness and confidence of your presence that we might be able to live with calmness and satisfaction with one another. Amen.

1980, 8 July.

Oh God what a day! So exasperating for some; so exhausting for many. Things that should have gone right didn't and things not counted on had to be dealt with. But, that's the way it is, isn't it? There is no victory without the perpetual vigilance of preparation and persistent skill and determination.

So we learned anew for the thousandth time that the only way we are ready for the challenge is the grueling ordeal of practice. Some of us learn faster and some slower but because we are human beings we all learn that the time of crisis is too late for acquiring the basic skills, courage and stamina to become victorious.

How humiliating it is in our personal lives when our "bore is fouled"; people come unhinged when they discover their impotency. Preserve us, God, from the destructive experiences of bore-fouled lives.

We admire the great works of art, literature and music because they seem so simple, so natural, so inevitable, so right. When we know the artist we know that his naturalness came only because he was faithful in the repetitious, exhausting and often monotonous exercises which enhanced his art.

Since human life is the highest form of art grant us the love of the art of life which convinces us of the value of practice. While it may not lead to perfection, may it at least lead to the rightness of doing what we must as if we do it because we may with confidence and increasing satisfaction. Amen.

1980, 10 July.

Dear Lord, there are a lot of hurting people in our world. Even if we are not moved by the plight of starving children or suffering old people in far off places because we feel there is little we can do for them there is so much hurt closer to us. Because we know the hurt of separation we can feel for those persons who are hostages of an insane regime or those Sailors and Marines in the Indian Ocean or those on regular deployments which are their lot.

But, even here on our ship there are a lot of hurting people -- people who hurt from the shock of death, or the anguish of disappointment; married men whose marriages are falling apart and threatening to tear them apart; disillusioned men who are disappointed in themselves and in other people. Oh God, keep us from becoming indifferent or insensitive to the hurts of others, especially our shipmates.

Life is hard enough for any person. Keep us from deliberately making it harder by hard-hearted or thoughtless disregard of the hurts of others. Give us enough confidence in one another that we share one another's pain and enough faith in You that we know that You are always ready to keep us steady when the bitterness of life blows hard. When we walk through the valley of shadows or toss about in the trough of broken dreams help us to look up and hear again "my grace is sufficient for your every need." Amen.

1980, 14 July.

Eternal God, once more we have gone to sea. Once more we leave those we love behind but never far from us in our thoughts and prayers. We are ever aware that we have chosen a life as rhythmical as the sea itself. We know life's fullness as the swell of the sea -- and the emptiness. We are acutely aware that our lives, like the water around us that rises for a moment, falls swiftly enough again into the eternal sea. So for a moment in your vast eternity we stand apart only to become again in time a part of the whole. May we, oh God, make the most of it. Keep us from the provincial despair that because we are not everything we are nothing.

You have created us in your image and set us in this time and this place to reflect your glory. May the way we do our work and live with one another be an offering of gratitude to You for having chosen us for so great a challenge and so responsible a task as life together on this ship. Amen.

1980, 15 July.

Dear Lord, we surely do misunderstand each other. I guess it's because we are different people with different backgrounds, different interests, different abilities and different objectives.

The wool pullers make a big hit while the less flashy are tuned out. What a powerful truth there is in realizing that only when a person has mastered himself can he freely and willingly serve other people. Grant us the patience, discipline and determination to master our lives, by your grace, so that we won't have to b.s. our way trying to get recognition or control. Make us honest with ourselves so that we can speak and act truthfully with one another. Amen.

1980, 16 July.

Eternal God, never have we known a more dedicated and genuinely concerned group of men working together than the company of this ship. So tonight we ask a special blessing on all those who sincerely seek to discharge their duties as leaders of men in a manner that at one and the same time seeks the highest technical performance, military smartness and human welfare.

We have heard often that from the man who has been given most in *leadership responsibility is expected the highest accountability. What a tremendous challenge and what an incredible reward when work well done is recognized and calls forth deeper commitment. What personal satisfaction there is in support from those to whom we are responsible and respect from those responsible to us.*

As we come to the close of the day, even in our weariness, may we be able to know the inner joy of having done our best. You are a great and loving God and have created us for greatness and human concern. Make us restless, Oh God, with any life which doesn't find its ultimate satisfaction in placing our lives in your care and keeping and sets us free from pettiness. We believe You have called us, the men of the PELELIU, to be the finest ship in our Navy. Grant us the religious commitment to achieve our goal so far as it is in our power and your grace. Amen.

1980, 17 July.

Before the Evening Prayer let me call your attention to a special ceremony we will have tomorrow at 1230 on the hangar-deck. It is in observance of POW-MIA Day which this year is Friday, 18 July. All men not on watch are expected to attend. Let us pray.

God of mercy and compassion we are aware tonight that some people suffer terribly so that others may enjoy even the negative freedom to complain about life's inconveniences and displeasures. Life is so easy for us even when it is hard when we compare the humiliation and deprivation of prisoners of war, hostages, or persons missing in action. We complain about what we eat or how frequently. For them there was never enough even of things that are sickening to us. We know how hard it is to do our job when we don't get enough sleep; they were often beaten to keep them from finding release from their pain and suffering in sleep. What horrors they endured; what heartache was the constant companion of their families. There are still some who hope against all measurable odds that their sons, husbands, fathers may return from missing in action. For those who died as prisoners of war, for those who are listed as missing in action, for our hostages in Iran whose humiliating imprisonment seems interminable, we offer You our prayers of respect. For those prisoners of war who survived their torturous ordeal and returned and who have become witnesses to the power of faith in You, oh God, and in man's indomitable spirit, we offer You our prayers of gratitude. Amen.

1980, 22 July.

God we take so much for granted and then something happens in our lives and we become aware of how important persons or things or experiences are. How fortunate we are to have been born in such an age as this. To be sure, it is a perilous and precarious age and the threat of death, destruction, even global annihilation are always with us even if we succeed for a while in pushing thoughts of them aside.

We realize the world is not a just and equitable place and there is much misery and suffering and bitterness and hatred and people taking advantage of one another. But God it is a grandly challenging age in which we have the means of communication and travel and resources to help ease other peoples pain or sorrow.

Sometimes there isn't a lot we can do to make much of a difference; but how can we live with ourselves if we don't try? Goodness and kindness, encouragement and hope are infectious. We can make a difference when we trust in You as our strength and joy. And it appears as sure as any other principle of order and life that when we offer our best to one another we not only enjoy the satisfaction of a better feeling about who we are but give to others along the way hope and acceptance and understanding. Thank You God for those things in life which we too often take for granted. When we become aware of them we are better at least for a while because of the contagious power of gratitude. Amen.

1980, 23 July.

Eternal God life seems to be a rhythm of constancy and change; both are needed. Without order, direction, purpose, schedules we could go nowhere nor could we accomplish anything together. Only when there is clarity and concurrence of purpose and procedure are we able to receive the benefits of success. But sometimes change becomes the order to which we respond and through which we grow. Tonight as we reflect on the day we thank You for its satisfactions. There were things we could have done better so we pray for forgiveness where our negativism or carelessness caused someone else a problem.

Give us each the gift we need. If we delight so much in change that we are heedless of the hard work of stabilizing our lives give us patience, perseverance, and endurance. If we are so welded to constancy that we become brittle or lose our perspective then open us up to the freedom of the new and unexpected.

Grant a night of well-earned rest to those whose labors are set aside for a while. To those who must stand the watches of the night grant vigilance and peace. To all of us on the morrow grant a joyous and thankful spirit we pray. Amen.

1980, 31 July.

Dear Lord God we are thankful that once again we may pause either as we prepare to rest or as we continue our work to thank You for your love and care. The situations of life make us often painfully aware that even the strongest among us can't go it alone.

We have a special prayer tonight for a select group of our shipmates. As is true so often many are called but few are chosen. We rejoice tonight with those few from the PELELIU who have been chosen to cross that extraordinary line from first class petty officer to chief petty officer in the Navy. We are glad for them and their families for the recognition and advantages it brings. We pray that they may enjoy exercising even more adequately those outstanding qualities of leadership which have been acknowledged by their peers in selecting them as chiefs. We share the disappointment of those who placed but didn't win, for it is a terribly hard thing to come in second when your goal is first.

Give them confidence in themselves and the ability to do well what they must do to accept the present and prepare for the future.

We offer also a special prayer for all chiefs and senior chiefs of our ship grateful for their years of experience and dedication. Enable them to set the highest example, offer the greatest encouragement and render the most positive service among us. Renew them constantly so that they may continue always as models worthy of our fullest admiration and respect. Grant us all now rest and peace. Amen.

1980, 1 August at anchor off Camp Pendleton, California.

Eternal God each night at sea we have the awesome responsibility of offering to You prayers on behalf of our shipmates, prayers of gratitude for special groups and persons. We seek to express on behalf of all of us prayers of confidence and gratitude. Yet, we are aware that life is not always special. For more than we care to admit there is no outstanding achievement, no glory, no acclaim. There is the incessant demand of the ordinary tasks of everyday.

We fasten our eyes on the spectacular either in the past or some yet unrealized future. Like Ham and Clov, actors in a play [*Waiting for Godot*], we carry on that dialogue: "Do you believe in life to come?" and hear the bitter-sweet reply, "Yes, mine always was."

Like children who believe there is something big about to happen we push into the future the confrontation with our own responsibility for who we are. So in our own separate ways we cope.

Shake us loose from escape into the future which keeps us from affirming the present. As wise men of old so often proclaimed help us to become wise enough to know and believe now is the day of wholeness. While we like the prophet of old discover there is no heavenly encounter in earthquake, wind and fire let us also like the prophet discover You in the still small voice within.

Like the poet [Gerard Manley Hopkins] give us grace to see Christ in ten thousand faces -- faces so much like our own and yet so different, faces that wear the marks of personal failure, disappointment, guilt or tragedy but faces which sometimes also reflect the glory and goodness of lives well lived.

While we may not be the same in color or achievement, or any of the marks that set men apart, help us to accept our humanity as a good if not always a glorious bond so that we bear one another's sorrows and share one another's joys and are thereby set free to be our own best selves.

Come to us in the stillness of a calm and confident life that we may echo your affirmation that because You have made it life is good. Amen.

1980, 3 August en-route to Seattle, Washington for SEAFAIR.

Dear Lord God how nice it is to have a day of rest. From ancient times You have given to man a Sabbath day of rest. You knew what we sometimes learn only with difficulty that we have to back off from the affairs and activities of everyday to keep our perspective and our sanity. We are so often unable to see the trees for the forest. So we are grateful when we may stop for a while to enjoy life.

We are grateful tonight for our cooks who provided the cook-out. Not only did they give that extra measure of service to provide enjoyable food for us but did it cheerfully adding to the pleasure. We thank You too for our shipmates who entertained us with their talents. Their music and comedy was a welcomed relief and recreation.

We thank You also for the freedom we enjoy to worship You when we desire and praise You for your clearest expression of your love to us in Jesus Christ. As You have refreshed us by extra sleep or worship or the picnic or music and laughter so we praise You for your never ending gifts of love. Accept our thanks at the end of this important day. Amen.

1980, 4 August.

Eternal God today's experiences make us grateful for this large and magnificent ship. As we watched the ships beside and aft of us rising from the water with immodestly exposed keel falling unceremoniously beneath spray drenched bow we were glad for the sailors who ride those ships and must endure the nausea and the embarrassment.

Our lives are like ships. There are different roles to play and jobs to be done by different types of vessels. The large ship can effectively accomplish what the smaller craft is neither designed nor equipped to do. Different lives like different ships make different contributions. Some lives are magnifi cent, grand, and expansive and appear to ride calmly through rough seas of personal tragedy, family distress, social, political, or financial upheaval. Other lives toss a lot and look as if they will come out of their element. Like Job they appear to get so sick of it all that they wish they could die. But somehow they ride out the conflict, sorrow, pain, and turbulence and wearily reach port.

As we make our individual voyages through life keep us steady. Though greatness may not be our personal lot even in our smallness may we faithfully run our course confident that as You have made us seaworthy so You will lead us to a safe harbor. Amen.

1980, 5 August in the Pacific Ocean the night before reaching port in Seattle, Washington for SEAFAIR.

Eternal God we look forward to another new liberty port with memories of Panama and Mexico, San Diego and Long Beach. Those were new and exciting places for many of us -- part of the adventure we signed up for. Now we have another opportunity to be proud of our ship and increase goodwill for our Navy, to stir new respect and positive feelings for our Nation. This remarkable crew of the PELELIU has already an enviable reputation. May it become even better. Let each one of us enjoy the pleasures of this liberty in a way which will let the memories we take with us be as satisfying as the experiences themselves.

Make us as proud of one another when we leave Seattle as we are as we enter. Let neither carelessness nor callousness blind us to the privileged responsibilities we have to ourselves, to those we love, and to our shipmates. Amen.

1980, 11 August in the Pacific Ocean en-route from Seattle, Washington to homeport Long Beach, California.

Gracious God we are grateful for our liberty in Seattle. Each of us found what he was looking for. For some there was friendship, renewed or begun. For most there was joyous hospitality often unexpected. We thank You God for the freedom to be ourselves; to seek and to find the release and relaxation we prefer or enjoy. What a great, wonderful God You are.

What a grand company of shipmates You have given to all of us on the PELELIU. We pray that You will continually help us to accept one another just as we are. We are glad we may love one another without the narrow necessity of imposing on each other our own personal values or morals or religious beliefs and commitments.

Grant, oh Lord, strength sufficient for the tasks which are ours where each man's work contributes to the successful accomplishment of our common mission. And grant by your grace forgiveness equal to our need, the ability to accept your acceptance of us and rest and peace through the night and always. Amen.

1980, 12 August.

Eternal God how often do we become aware of the countless ways our lives depend on other people. That dependence is sometimes visible as when an electrician repairs a heater or an HT unstops a toilet. It is less visible when the quartermasters plot our course or the operation specialists survey the contacts.

It is not often noticed when that influence is through books and the stories, talks, insights of authors. There is that long ago religious influence of childhood prayers: "Now I lay me down to sleep I pray Thee Lord my soul to keep," or "God is great, God is good, let us thank him."

While we grow in every other way as men, may we grow also in greater appreciation for others' seen and unseen gifts to our lives and for a fuller understanding of those childhood truths of your greatness and goodness on which we depend even if we don't acknowledge them. Amen.

1980, 13 August.

God our Father there was good news today. One of our men got word he *has a son and that mother and baby are doing fine. How happy he was! And how happy we are to share with him! Now he has the most awesome responsibility you place in human hands -- to become in fact a good father. Each of us bears from our own mother and father marks so deep that they can't be erased.*

Tonight we thank You for parents. For our own parents who left their imprint so clearly on us. We thank You for every good influence they had on us becoming who we are and pray your forgiveness for those influences which we had to struggle against. In most cases it wasn't from evil intent that they failed to measure up to their own best ideals. If they did the best they knew how and loved us what more could they do?

We pray that each one of us on the PELELIU who is a father may tonight pause for his own prayer of gratitude for his sons or daughters. Give us the wisdom to hold them close but not too close, the faith to share our highest hopes for them without condemning them to a life-long quest of trying to measure up to our expectations, and a love consistent with our own natures that keeps them steady in good times and bad. Amen.

1980, 14 August before arriving in homeport Long Beach, California from Seattle.

Eternal God we near the end of this particular journey. The Marines will return to their units and resume their regular training. We ask you to bless them and their leaders. Make them proud of the honorable traditions of their Corps. Place in each of them the desire and the will to be a Marine of valor, courage, and honor.

Others will leave us too. Already a few have left for humanitarian reasons but now Doctor Guzley leaves for a new assignment. We thank you for his contributions to our welfare and his enthusiastic involvement in the life of our ship. We pray You may favor him with increasingly compassionate service in the ministry of healing in the spirit of the Great Physician.

Many of our company will take leave soon after we get into port. Some to enter into the new relationship of marriage, some to await the birth of their child, some to try to patch up ailing marriages, some to regain perspective. For all of them in their special needs and hopes we pray. Sustain them in their accomplishments of what they either desire to or must do.

Continue to deepen our awareness that You are the source and strength of our life. In your will may our sense of community and our commitment to one *another grow for the good of all and the fulfillment of each. Amen.*

1980, 2 September in the SOCAL operating area of the Pacific Ocean.

Eternal God as we return again to sea we are grateful for the privilege of prayer. As Jesus, our Lord, cautioned there is danger in prayer. As he told men long ago so he would say to us today beware of practicing your piety before men; don't be like the hypocrites who love to stand on street corners and draw attention to themselves. They have their reward. People notice them and talk about them and they praise one another. Let us hear him when he says, "When you pray do it quietly, without calling attention to yourself and God who sees the secret devotion of a true heart will reward you openly."

Father how great the rewards to those who find the secret place of their lives a sanctuary from the corruptions to which we are all prone. As the poet has said, "To every man there opens a way and ways and a way and some men choose the high way and some men choose the low, but in between on the misty flats the rest drift to and fro." [John Oxenham] Give us drifters the courage to choose the higher way. Let us without fanaticism or fanfare be faithful to the

93

gift of life we have been given and return it to You a service to others. This is our prayer. Amen.

1980, 3 September.

Eternal God, our Father, on behalf of this incredibly fine company of naval personnel we offer You our prayer of gratitude this night. There is such a rich diversity of gifts and an amazing breadth of needs. Some have been blessed with an infectious sense of humor that lifts and brightens our days, some have a gift of compassion and are able to sense and share other's hurts and sorrows and needs, some have a gift of insight and understanding and patiently share with us knowledge that enables us to do our work better or see things more clearly. Some have the amazing power to see problems as opportunities and obstacles as challenges. Some are able to take the ordinary experiences of life and treat them with such integrity that they attain an extraordinary quality. Some have a gift of perseverance which keeps on where weaker men would give up and challenge us to give our best. For these varied gifts we thank You. Enable each of us to use his special gifts for the good of others to your glory. Amen.

1980, 4 September.

Dear Lord God every night in evening prayers we pray as if we all were going to sleep. But every day we become increasingly aware that's not the case for many on our ship. Men will stand watches throughout the night. The bridge will be skillfully manned, a safe course will be plotted and steered; in CIC scopes will be scanned and objects noted; in the galley mid-rats will be faithfully served; in the engineering spaces consoles, dials, and gauges will be competently monitored and adjusted; high above us signalmen will search the dark to keep us free from harm; in radio messages will be dutifully transmitted and received; forward and aft lookouts will keep their lonely vigil. Men will awaken from a short sleep to assume their watch and when that watch is ended will grab a little more sleep before beginning all over again another day's activities.

For those guardians of the night on whose alertness and dedication all our lives depend we offer our grateful prayers and sincere appreciation. We are amazed, oh God, at the unusually positive attitude and demeanor of these our shipmates.

We may not always choose what we must do but we may always choose how well we will do it. Give us the desire and the will, the strength and the purpose to do well what we must do throughout our lives. Amen.

1980, 5 September prayer on the night when return to homeport Long Beach was delayed until the next day.

God it has been another one of those days! There was terrible crushing sorrow for one of us. Death the awful enemy took away one whose love meant life itself to him How many already in our short life together have felt this awful onslaught of death? Heartache and heartbreak are such regular companions of our crew. Yet, they are strong men who never cease to astound us. When they come to the end of their rope, they tie a knot and hang on.

It was a day of disappointment too. Many worked so hard for so long at their challenging task only to have it completed anticlimactically through no fault of their own.

There was the disappointment of not being able to return as scheduled to those they love. But, they are remarkable men. They don't have to pretend it doesn't matter, or they don't care, or they are unmarked by such events! They can admit realistically it affects them because they believe in what they are

96

doing and in their faithfulness in doing it.

We know, oh God, sailors have always known disappointment not of a few hours delay but often of days, weeks, months. This will ever be the lot of those who follow the sea.

For those who experience the agony of death or disappointment let your peace which passes all understanding guard their hearts and minds in Christ Jesus, our Lord, in whose spirit we pray. Watch over and care for those we love now and evermore. Amen.

1980, 16 September final contract trials and INSURVE Board visit.

Eternal God as we offer our evening prayers tonight we reflect with gratitude on those experiences in our short life as a ship when we have done well those things which were ours to do, those times when we have been encouraged by the spontaneous praise of those who acknowledged the enthusiasm, dedication, and pride of this incredible crew. From the beginning we have been blessed with extraordinary leadership and high expectations. You have cared for us in a very special way. To us much has been given; from us much is required. We are glad for the demanding challenges of this finest of ships.

We pray a special prayer tonight for the men and women who have come to share with us the richness of their knowledge, the uniqueness of their expertise, and the candor of their valued perspective. We thank You that their coming is a fitting opportunity to test ourselves. Their positive approach and evident desire to assist us in further becoming what we believe we are destined to be is no small gift. Make us responsive to their guidance for overcoming our weaknesses even as You enable them to be appreciative of our strengths.

Grant to the men of the PELELIU the serenity of confident preparation and commendable performance. To those on whose vital watches of the night our lives depend grant alertness and strength. To all others grant a calm and restful sleep as fit preparation for a new day offering ample occasions for giving the best that we are to one another. Amen.

1980, 29 September the first night at sea after the death of one of our shipmates.

Eternal God once more we set out to sea, once more we feel the challenges of our tasks, once more we leave behind those we love and quietly resolve to come back again better men than when we left. But this time it is different. For now all of us have entered into the shocked dismay of senseless death. Often enough we have mourned with our shipmates who have walked through the valley of the shadow of death; fathers and mothers and sisters and brothers deaths have left them disconsolate.

Now death's horror, so close at hand, has left us with the sickening ache in the pit of our stomachs forcing anew the insistent question, "What's it all about?" To whom can we go for our answer? Where do we find our consolation? Where is our peace and serenity? Where shall we find our rest amidst the restlessness?

This night we pray for your comfort for Harry Selfridge's family in their great loss. We pray that the peace that passes understanding may keep their hearts and minds in Christ Jesus. We pray that in their emptiness there may come awareness that underneath are your everlasting arms. Give us grace to remember all that was good and noble, to lay aside what it is not ours to determine, to leave in your eternal wisdom and love questions we cannot answer as we set ourselves with firmer *dedication to make the most of the life that is ours. Preserve us from weakness.*

You are the Living God. Indeed You are the God of the living. So let each of us live his life with integrity. Give us power to be faithful in little things -- the work we do, the commitments we make, the trust that others place in us, the encouragement and hope that is ours to share so that we need never fear the terror of meaninglessness. Even if we are not called to be heroes let us by your grace be heroic in the faithfulness of our ordinary and everyday affairs.

We rest ourselves in You this night that we might be refreshed and renewed for every new tomorrow which comes as your kind gift. Amen.

1980, 30 September in the Pacific Ocean en-route to Hawaii for first major exercise (RIMPAC READEX).

Oh God there are days when big events occur and we see life on a grand scale or days when crises drive us to the extremities of our own resources and we are left with nowhere to turn but to You. There are times when we are fascinated by the awesome prospects of what might lie over the horizon of our world. But most days are regular days un-distinguished by great sadness or great joy; days when there is nothing to make either the physical or the spiritual adrenaline flow.

We are amazed at how well most people handle crises. When the stakes are high most men play a pretty good game. But what of the daily contests when there are no bands or cheerleaders or roaring crowds, no visible life-threatening dangers or vicious enemies to defeat? It is then that we need to be athletes of the spirit who stretch our inner muscles, stay with unglamorous discipline, remember the victories of the past and anticipate the conflicts of the future. It is then we pray, "Lord, it's just another day but if I let go of the strength and confidence, the standards of excellence, the quiet awareness that what I am I am because I am yours then how can I possibly play the game with satisfaction either for myself, my teammates, or the side-line spectators?"

Let us keep on keeping on without yielding to the temptation to have to be keyed up all the time or let down if there is neither the thrill of success nor the disturbance of defeat. Keep us from being so anxious about the big tomorrows that we lose the strength of the little todays. Amen.

1980, 1 October.

Dear God our prayers are a barometer of the spiritual climate of our ship. When there is a positive mood of confidence and hope we are filled with gratitude and joy; when the mood turns toward the slackening of will we transmit unsettled expressions of disappointment.

We offer You prayers for the things close at hand and most evident. There is so much to note in everyday -- an awful lot of friendliness and kindness which is true and genuine. In calling attention to these virtues we seek their growth. But we are not blind to the darker side of our lives. "Sin is ever crouching at the door" as the wise man long ago said waiting to pounce upon us leading us to reprehensible action.

We are baffled by the ability of men who know one another intimately to lie to each other or steal from one another or vandalize what is the common property of us all or to treat a shipmate with disdain or to trample on the sensitivities of someone else by trying to bullshit or con one another.

We know there is not a man among us who is not capable of evil. But we thank You God that most of us most of the time are able to live on a higher plain. We thank You for the saints among us, not the holy men who are unstained by sin but men whose *dominant motif is gratitude. What a rich array of gratitude blesses this ship.*

There is not a day goes by that we are not more acutely aware of the skill and gifts of our shipmates whether our very able doctor and corpsmen, or deck hands or ship-handlers or engineers or operation personnel or airmen or those who supply our material needs. Keep us from taking one another for granted. Enable us always to take one another for gratitude in the spirit of the Christ in whose name we pray. Amen.

1980, 2 October.

Gracious God what joy there is when good news comes and it is well deserved. What excitement when right decisions are made and honor comes to those to whom honor is due. Tonight we offer You our heart-felt thanks for the selection of our Executive Officer to the rank of Captain. As we have sorrowed with those who sorrow so now we praise You for the privilege of rejoicing with him who rejoices.

We have one other special prayer tonight Dear Lord. The generosity of this ship astounds us. Not only is there visible concern for children and the elderly in work done and yet to be done, there is the more difficult compassion of caring for others whom we will probably never see through gifts to the Combined

Federal Campaign. It is no small measure of achievement for our men to average over twenty dollars a man for others and provide so large an amount for agencies to care for those in need. It is a task well deserving of commendation for Warrant Officer Bonner and the key-men who worked so faithfully. We hear Jesus our Lord saying again, "In as much as you have given to one of the least of these my brethren you have done goodness to me." And we rejoice, for goodness endures. Amen.

1980, 3 October.

Dear God let's have a prayer for the little people tonight. Not the short ones or thin ones or scrunched up ones; but the men whose work is not in the limelight or spotlight. Those who sometimes get the idea that because they are not singled out they are not appreciated. While they may go unheralded or un-applauded help them to feel that we know that if they were not doing their work well none of us would succeed.

While we often "praise famous men and our fathers who gave us birth", as the biblical writer said we know there is praise for every man who with quiet undistinguished dignity performs his tasks.

We all need the encouragement of Atta Boys and Bravo Zulus. But help us to find a deeper reason for our work. Let those who can like Brother Lawrence polish their pots and pans for the glory of God. Let those who can do the laundry or PMS equipment because if they didn't things would be in an awful mess. Let those who can feel the assurance that there are no insignificant tasks only some men who do them insignificantly. And let all know the calm assurance that we are all called upon not so much to excel as to persevere to the best of our unique abilities.

Grant now to us a night of rest through sleep however short and strength sufficient for our assigned or chosen labors. Amen.

1980, 9 October RIMPAC READEX off Hawaii. During this operation we became acutely aware of the role of the PELELIU's Ombudspersons capably chaired by Sandy Stafford in supporting our families when we are away.

Eternal God it was a demanding day. Our Marines executed their carefully planned and rehearsed events with armored vehicles and helicopters challenged by wind and waves. With orderly precision they carried out the debarkation of troops. They learned new lessons as they performed old tasks. All of us began to see a faint glimmer of what it might be like when we undertake our primary mission.

We experienced the necessity of Sailors and Marines mutually supporting one another. What a great ship this is even as she rolls and strains. What an even greater crew as they stretch to meet new demands. And in the midst of it all there is the reality of ties with home.

We thank you, oh God, for the compassionate humanity of those who must make decisions in response to human needs. Tonight we pray a special prayer for our families and those who support them in our absence. The flood of AMCROSS messages makes us aware of their dependence on us. We are grateful for the helpful and readily available resources of Navy Relief, Red Cross, Ombudsmen, Wives Club and friends. We are glad there are persons ready, willing, and able to help in times of need -- persons at home and persons aboard ship.

May we be secure tonight in your love which is our strength. Keep us from the misguided notion that other men's emergencies result from their bothersome weakness. In quiet confidence let us rest and work to make life better by sharing *one another's cares rather than adding to one another's burdens. Amen.*

1980, 16 October.

Dear Father God soon the whine of helicopter engines will have ceased after a long and exhausting day for pilots and crews. The clanging of tie-down chains will stop as they are dropped again into their slots. Crash and salvage equipment will be put away. A tried and tested Air Department will wrap up its longest sustained operation with a sense of satisfaction.

All will be still again as we steam through the night. For your benevolent protection we are grateful. Every new exercise brings a greater sense of gratitude for the skill and devotion of so remarkable a crew. How gently You lead us. How kindly You are to open our eyes to your loving care in the ordinary experiences of men knowing and respecting one another more and more. How rich the expressions of faith as they appear in varied forms.

We marvel at the wonders of man's inventiveness and genius but marvel even more that You have created us with a consciousness that remembers and learns, that ponders and probes, that anticipates and plans. Let the long search lead us eventually closer to You for then we will recognize our closeness

to one another as brothers and be glad.
Amen.

1980, 20 October A Tiger Cruise en-route to homeport Long Beach after exercises in Hawaii.

As most of you know it is our privilege to have Chaplain Kane at sea with us. We invite all who will to join him in the celebration of Roman Catholic Mass in the Library each day at 1120. Now join me for the evening prayer.

Eternal God what a flood of emotions overtake us as we set out to sea again. There is such excitement and joyous anticipation of returning to our homes and families. For some there is the awareness that this is their last cruise aboard the PELELIU for they will have gone on to other assignments before we set sail again. For all of us there is the awareness that we enter a new dimension of our life together. We go back to enter into what is for any ship a difficult time. We earnestly pray that the confidence and goodwill that has accumulated like a finely wrought work of art may help to sustain us in the tedious days ahead.

We carry also the emotion of having been in one of the most indelibly imprinted places in our nation's history. [USS ARIZONA Memorial] We stood at attention rendering honors to the memories of men who like ourselves bore the honorable title of sailors in our

Nation's Navy and for which honor they died. In so short a time the course of history has moved with such swiftness. We pray for forgiveness of the horrors of war and the destruction that like a blinding rage calls out the best and the worst in us. We thank You that the animosities that ravage have been turned into the alliances that set about creating new worlds, that swords have been beaten into plow-shears for better world order.

And there are the happy emotions of having some of our sons and fathers with us. We welcome them as representatives of all those whom we hold dear. May they have a good voyage, the memories of which will last a life-time.

There is so much to pray but You know that already. Hear the deep prayers of every man's heart. Grant forgiveness for our sins, absolution of our guilt, serenity to our troubled hearts, strength for a better life and a sense of gratitude for the privilege of the life we share together on this good ship. Amen.

1980, 22 October.

Eternal God sometimes we pray for little things of everyday. Sometimes we pray for special persons, places, or events. Sometimes we pour out our deepest gratitude for the goodness of life a divine gift offered by human hands. Our prayers are conversations with You about our life together on the PELELIU.

Tonight Israel's prophet shouts at us, "let justice roll down like waters and righteousness like a mighty stream." And what is justice? Many have tried to teach us. From at least one perspective it is when each man contributes what he can for the good of the whole.

It is a grave injustice when men bring shame, dishonor, and disgrace upon the whole crew. How quickly the reputation of hundreds can be damaged by the injustice and violence of a handful. We all know the temptation to injustice which paces the cages of our hearts. Thanks be to You Lord God that so wild a beast is tamed by a sense of honor, integrity, self-worth, and respect. Violence is a raging fire soon out of control. It is easily fanned by the chilling winds of men who stand passively by doing nothing. Have mercy upon us not because we are models of justice and naturally merciful men but because You are a just God whose mercy is from everlasting to everlasting.

How right the struggling saint was when he declared, "Man becomes like what he loves." [St. Augustine] If we love violence we become violent men. If we take upon ourselves to settle our own affairs by illegitimate means we become outlaws and anarchists. If we slur and slander one another by careless disregard or prejudice we become animals. We pray for the restraint and courage to prove ourselves men.

What no sense of shame keeps us from doing, let no cowardly conscience prevent us from confessing. Let no fear of ourselves or others make us indifferent and irresponsible. Help us to put away bitter thoughts so that they do not lead us to even more bitter actions.

Father forgive us and cleanse us and restore within each of us our commitment to justice even if we are not yet mature enough for the greater blessings of brotherhood. Amen.

1980, 24 October prior to entering homeport Long Beach to begin Post Shakedown Availability (PSA) in the shipyard.

Eternal God no prayer we have offered on behalf of our beloved crew has been as difficult as this we pray tonight. As our brother in Christ prayed last night, change is our constant companion calling forth from us resources too deep for our own limited abilities. We have admirably met challenging changes that pushed one another out of the way. Now we face a challenge greater than all the rest. There will be no relief of days and nights at sea stretching our skills or strengthening our faith. There will be no evening prayers echoing our daily experiences in the light of your loving care.

What shall we pray tonight: "father save us from this time of our lives." No for that is both a foolish and a futile prayer. For none of us has the power to change the course of our common life. Rather God we pray like our Lord, "Father if it be possible let this trial pass from me but if it is not possible then not what I desire but what You will be done." As men of faith we believe it is your will that we live at peace with one another. Blessed are the peacemakers.

For whatever reason each of us has chosen to be a sailor -- to subject himself to authority, to be accountable to those above us and responsible to those below us.

We are not holy men, oh God, but we are men created in your image. Jesus told his disciples, "For their sake I sanctify myself." Was that a dedication of which only he was capable? We believe not. Rather it was one of life's deepest truths. If there is no one to whom we are accountable we quickly count for nothing. If there is no one whose welfare is our responsibility we easily become irresponsible.

So tonight we pray whatever our position on the PELELIU that the time that awaits us may draw us close to You not because we have no one else to whom we may go but because turning to You we then know which way to turn. Though our public prayers will cease for a while let this be all the more reason to find appropriate ways for our private conversation with you to grow.

Let us like the poet see "Christ in ten thousand faces" in unlikely places. Search us and try us, Oh Lord, and see if there be any wicked way in us; blot out our sins, purge us and cleanse us. On this special night we pray a prayer I learned from one from I learned much: "Come Holy Spirit come. Come as the wind and cleanse, come as the fire and burn, come as the light and reveal. Convict, convert, consecrate until we are wholely thine." [Nels F.S. Ferre] For then , dear Father, we shall truly belong to one another. Amen.

1981, 7 July sea trials in the SOCAL operating area of the Pacific Ocean near the end of PSA.

God it has been such a long time since we shared these special moments of evening prayer. Many new shipmates have come aboard since we last set sail many months ago. For some this is their first venture on the mysterious and alluring sea. We are grateful for the privilege of reestablishing our sense of pride as PELELIU sailors. As we experience once again the awesome exhilaration of being at sea may we reaffirm our confidence in one another.

How good it is to feel the smooth and steady hum of giant engines moving us, to rely once more on the sure calculations of those who chart and plot our course, to respond joyfully to the persistence and tenacity of those whose labors have brought us to so significant a time in our life together.

As You have cared for us through the dogged difficulties of our yard period so may You reinvigorate us for the successful resumption of the tasks which give meaning to our lives as Sailors. Sustain us by your love that we might properly care for one another by the faithful performance of the work each of us has to do. Grant us rest and peace and the re-creation of life and spirit which comes from the conviction that having been created in your image we are destined for lives of meaning and fullness. Amen.

1981, 8 July.

Eternal God we are grateful for a time for evening prayer and for the positive response of our shipmates. We seek to become aware for even so brief a time that life is your gift, that we had nothing to do with when and where and to whom we would be born. But life is also an achievement. We take what we are given and fashion it and make it into something useful, productive, and creative. What we do with our skills brings us appreciation of others whether it is a delicious meal well prepared, a message clearly transmitted, a helicopter successfully flown, lines rightly cast off - whatever the achievement we take pride in it and are glad.

You give us even greater material to work with. You say here is your life, you are free to make of it what you will. You can invest it. You can artistically refine it. You can expand it. You can waste it too if you like.

God we thank You for so terrible a freedom. And we thank You that on the PELELIU there are so many men whose playful seriousness about life, whose genuine concern for others, whose sense of humor and integrity, whose satisfaction in what they do and who they are is an inspiration and a challenge. Whether we openly acknowledge it or not, oh God, we know that You have created us and set us free to become who we are and hold us accountable.

Grant us your grace as individuals to become the best men we are capable of being and as a ship to become a model of a humane naval unit caring for one another in such a way that each man is stronger and we as a whole are better because in your destiny and our freedom we take special meaning in being a part of the PELELIU. Amen.

1981, 9 July.

Dear God some of our company find themselves in a strange situation which happened surprisingly fast. It reminds us of the folk wisdom which says, "be careful what you wish for you might get it." Sometimes we burn with the conviction that we have to have something which we think is impossible to get, then when to our surprise we get it we either don't know what to do with it or we want to give it back, to call the whole thing off, to say "but I was only kidding." Even though we bring it on ourselves we have a hard time accepting it.

Maybe there is help for us in the oft used prayer of St. Francis of Assisi:

Lord make me an instrument of your peace.

Where there is hatred let me sow love;

Where there is injury, pardon;

116

Where there is doubt, faith;
Where there is despair, hope;
Where there is darkness, light;
And where there is sadness, joy.
O Divine Master grant that I may
not so much seek to be consoled as
to console;
To be understood, as to
understand;
To be loved, as to love;
For it is in giving that we receive.
It is in pardoning that we are
pardoned
And it is in dying that we are
born to eternal life.
May this prayer be for all of us a
comfort and a guide from weakness to
strength, from alienation to a closer
walk with You, oh God. Amen.

1981, 10 July Sea Trials continued beyond anticipated finish date.

Well God I really didn't expect to
be back up here this time talking with
You again on behalf of our PELELIU
people. Sure, we had been told that we
might not come in on Friday if the sea
trials were not complete but who wants to
believe that kind of talk. It isn't that we
mind. You know we love the sea and our
life together on the ship but still we're
disappointed. Some of our wives won't
get the word and they'll worry or get

mad, yes they'll get mad all right because we didn't come home when they thought we would or nobody called to tell them of the change in plans, or they've been puttin' up with the kids all week and were looking forward to a night out. Is it too much to ask that You somehow calm 'em down, increase their faith and trust, give 'em a little more patience, tolerance and understanding so that they won't be so nervous and upset. And by the way God, help us to remember when we get back to give them somebody's phone number so they can check with them next time we go out.

A couple of other things if we may God, give extra strength and stamina to our engineers who work so hard and long during these sea trials. Watch out and care for all the yard workers, technicians and ship riders who are with us. Keep our watch standers alert even while You give rest and peace to the rest of us who sleep through the night. Amen.

1981, 27 July in the SOCAL operating area of the Pacific Ocean.

Eternal God some days it seems all we do is go round and round like a dog chasing his tail until he tires of the game and runs off in some new direction. We look at others and say how thrilling it must be to find excitement in the commonplace or satisfaction in the ordinary. We sometimes wish the dull monotony or repeated experiences were touched by some bright mystery or some shining hope. We seek and do not find; we knock and no door opens. And then like some faint echo, some narrow sliver of light faith urges us on.

Faith, "the substance of things hoped for, the promise of things not seen" will not leave us alone. Like the desperate father responding to Jesus we answer back, "I am a man of faith, but accept my lack of faith." It is easy enough to have faith when life shouts out, "come on down" and we know the price is right and we have made the bid right on the money. But we need faith when we sit in our seats like some expectant would-be contestant and no one calls our name. We need faith when our circling lives like ships boring holes in the sea lose their ripples in the rise and swell of everyday.

Come to us God that we may come near to You. Walk with us so that the very seeking is our joy, the knowing is itself faith greater than our doubts or our weariness. Let faith be like the key which unlocks the door to a higher and better life with You with whom it all has its meaning, its purpose, its power and its peace. Amen.

1981, 28 July.

God we pray tonight focusing on today's big event. We are pleased to share the joy of those who did their work well and made us all proud of them. We acknowledge their success even as we share some of their disappointment. The success is far greater than the failure. It is really hard to make a perfect score whether firing guns or living life. We do pretty well if we get off a majority of successful rounds. We have reason to be proud when we do our best even if there are unexpended rounds. Even though we know not many have ever lived who fired a perfect score, we thank You that most of us are more often successful than not. There are some people who are outstanding, who make it all fit together, who have taken their bearings, found a clear range, and are convincingly human whether at slow or rapid fire.

Tonight on behalf of my shipmates I offer You our prayers of gratitude for those of the fabulous five's finest who will depart the ship before we set sail again. Some of them we will remember for as long as we value good humor, incredible devotion, incomparable loyalty, work well done and compassionate honesty. We wish we could name each one of them. You know them all and so do we.

Let them know how much we appreciate them and how we pray that you will bless their lives as they have blessed ours.

We offer a special prayer for our Executive Officer. Few men can be as open with others about their own strengths and weaknesses. It is so rare to find a man whose evident joy is to do everything in his power for the good of others. It is only occasionally that we find a man who enjoys the satisfaction of service more than the prominence of praise. We thank You for Paul Guay who has set a standard of integrity and excellence which is the hallmark of the PELELIU. Bless him and all that he does. God go with him and with all the others whose lives have enriched our life together on the PELELIU. Amen.

1981, 8 September.

Oh God sometimes we feel like such clods. Our friends share news with us of great disappointment and we either can't get anything to come out or what we do say sounds so stupid. Why is it so hard to talk about the things that mean most to us? We want to know each other but friendship is hard to cultivate. We want to be so tuned in to a few people that we hurt when they hurt or are really happy when they are happy. It isn't easy God. It is easy to know a lot of people casually. But it is hard to know anybody deeply enough to share life's big news.

We hear so much but listen so little. So much goes on around us yet we see so little of what goes on among us. Rather than pray for better mouths to speak with we pray for appropriate words worth speaking at the right time. Rather than praying for keener ears to hear with we pray for the power to hear what people are really trying to say to us. Rather than praying for inspiring or profound messages for uncomfortable times we pray for the strength and humility to say sincerely, "Dear friend, I know." Care for us through the night and always as by your grace we care for one another. Amen.

1981, 9 September.

Eternal God the tempo quickens with activities sharpening and fine-tuning our abilities and effectiveness. We become increasingly aware that performance depends not only on thorough planning but equally on persons dedicated to giving their best in executing those plans. Men cannot be coerced into performing well but men committed to supporting one another in common ventures give far more than anyone could ever demand.

We saw that again today as we have seen it from the beginning of our life together on the PELELIU. We saw it and were glad. We saw it and were grateful. We saw it and knew that what each of us does is important to all of us. It was a smooth evolution done by men who care; men for whom carelessness is unthinkable.

Where does such a rare spirit come from? We believe, our Father, it comes ultimately from You. You have chosen to place within each of us a strong sense of pride, a firm sense of integrity, a dedicated sense of contributing what we can for the good of all. Gratefully we thank You even as we pray for that constant renewal of strength and purpose to do all to your glory and for one another's good. Amen.

1981, 10 September.

Here we are again God - You and me and all these men listening in on our conversation. That's all right with me and I don't think You mind either. Usually our conversations are about everyday events with sometimes not so everyday meanings. Sometimes we talk about the things we have done or the things we have seen others do. Isn't it amazing that we see things differently depending upon whether we are doing or being done to. I'm sure, God, I see it a lot different when I'm getting chewed out than I do when I'm chewing on someone else.

When we act before considering how it might affect the other person we think of ourselves as decisive, bold, able to take charge, a defender of our own rights or protector of others. But when someone else is treating us that way we think of him as thoughtless, heartless, inconsiderate, unkind, a wild man.

You know God it reminds me of that delightful story by Soren Kierkegaard called, "What says the Fire Chief?" You know the one - where the Fire Chief is usually such a pleasant fellow speaking at civic clubs, smiling at people on the street, greeting them with a handshake as he goes, giving positive interviews to the press, making everybody around him happy. Then those same people see him at a fire and want to exchange pleasantries with him as they usually do. But to their shocked dismay he erupts like a volcano yelling at them to "get the hell out of the way" so that he can lead in fighting the fire.

Like the Fire Chief let us be men of civility in our ordinary lives and men of unashamed resolve when the fire needs putting out. And, oh God, let us know the difference between a smoke screen and a real fire. Amen.

1981, 28 September Rosh Hashanah,, the Jewish New Year.

God of Abraham, Isaac and Jacob, of Moses and David, of Amos, Micah, and Isaiah we welcome this New Year the 5,742nd of the Jewish calendar with deep gratitude for what has come to all of us by your creation and election of the Jews as your chosen people. From them we have gained a vision of society based on law and order, of community grounded in faith and covenant commitment, of family in which ritual and responsibility nurture one another. In their exodus they have given to us the burning belief that freedom even with struggle is a destiny better than slavery even with ease. In their exile they have given to us the heritage of hope beyond the security of home or happiness. In their insistence on Torah they have taught us that obedience is the true way to life fulfilled and satisfying. In their conviction that they were chosen to live out their lives as a witness to shalom, to peace, justice, righteousness, and loving-kindness we have come to affirm that all people everywhere are created in your image and that beneath all human history are your everlasting arms.

The gods of greed, ambition, lust, exploitative power, abuse and corruption become vain idols when with the Jews we proclaim, "Shema Israel adonai Elohainu, adonai ehad: Hear, oh Israel, the Lord our God is one God." We rejoice in our common humanity.

As we wish our Jewish shipmates Happy New Year, we renew our faith in You who art the same yesterday, today, and forever, the One Eternal God. Amen.

1981, 29 September.

Dear God there are prayers we offer on great themes, magnificent occasions, or historic experiences. They are prayers of elevated and literary speech. They are appropriate for the events.

Some among us offer prayers daily for all of us. There are those who do not go to sea with us but who undergird us with their prayers. We are grateful.

Prayer is such a mystery. Even though we don't know all we would like to know we know enough to believe prayer is as essential for our life together as fuel is for our engines, or food for our bodies, or lines for our mooring.

We pray in a lot of different ways. Some pray formally and religiously. Some don't think of what they do as prayer though surely it is. When the Apostle Paul admonished his readers to pray without ceasing he knew work always has to be done. Maybe he meant the very way we do our work is a prayer.

126

There were a lot of prayers on the PELELIU today and if we thank You for one specific prayer please know we are not ungrateful for others as well. There was a beautiful prayer offered by Comm and Personnel and Air and Supply and the Captain and the XO and so many others who responded genuinely to a deep human need of one of the least among us.

It is as if we hear you saying, "Well done good and faithful servants; in as much as you have taken care of one of the least of these my brethren you have done it unto me."

May we always offer You our prayers of service which are even more powerful than our prayers of words. Amen.

1981, 30 September   Evening prayer preempted due to refueling at sea.

1981, 1 October.

Eternal God what an enthusiastic group of men serve together on the PELELIU. There is always genuine excitement whenever any segment of our company succeeds at its task. Many of us have served in commands where this was not the case, where divisions and departments were actually glad when other people failed.

An increasing number of our crew are serving at sea for the first time. Maybe it is hard for them to realize how fortunate we all are that there is a spirit of cooperation and encouragement here. There are few persons, oh God, who don't carry around some care or burden which could easily defeat them. The remarkable thing is that most of our shipmates are able to handle their problems so well. There is so much to learn from one another. Greatness is contagious.

Let our lives reflect firm faith in every man's ability to respond positively to the challenges put to him. Even when what we do is not very glamorous, for instance when we are FSAs or compartment cleaners may we do it with faithfulness and good spirit which expresses our conviction that there are no tasks too small or menial for us. As Jesus has said, "he who is faithful in little tasks will be faithful when given greater things to do."

Help us to experience that joy and satisfaction which comes from each one of us doing his very best for the good of all of us. Amen.

1981, 5 October following burial at sea of the cremated remains of AKC Gordon Donald Anderson and SK3 Joseph Patrick Burke off the Southern California coast.

Eternal God no day is the same as any other, yet every day is the same. No life is the same as any other though every life is the same.

Today we experienced another first on the PELELIU. There have been so many. There will be many more.

We acknowledged the gift and responsibility of life as we engaged in a ceremony of death. We were proud as we are always proud of the men of the PELELIU. We knew neither of the men whose ashes we ceremoniously committed to the sea. Yet there was a kinship between us. We saw how small a man's physical remains are as they fell into the sea and were immediately swallowed up. We could not see what those men's lives had meant to their families and friends and nation. The son of one of them stood proud of his father and was so obviously influenced by him. The other had no one among us who knew him.

Yet as the poet has so rightly made known to us, "Don't ask for whom the bell tolls, it tolls for thee; no man is an island unto himself, each is a piece of the promontory; land washed into the sea." [John Donne]We did not have to ask for whom the volleys were fired as the notes of taps floated away on the ocean breezes. We knew.

We knew, oh God, that so long as men honor the dead they will not dishonor the living. So long as they feel the influence of one life on another no life can be insignificant. We thank You this night for the noble men of the PELELIU who were made even nobler by their honoring of men unknown but long to be remembered.

Grant us now rest and peace and a renewed sense of purpose as we live out our lives under the shadow of your all-encompassing care. Amen.

1981, 6 October day of the assassination of President Anwar Sadat of Egypt.

Men as most of you know by now, President Anwar Sadat, winner of the Nobel Peace Prize, died today victim of an assassin's bullets. I would like to share with you some of Anwar Sadat's thoughts from his autobiography, *In Search of Identity*:

This is the story of my life. . .
It is, I believe like every man's life, a journey in search of identity. Each step I have taken over the years has been for the good of Egypt, and has been designed to serve the cause of right, liberty, and peace. This is the image I have had of myself since childhood. Now, as the landscape of my life unfolds before

my eyes, can I claim that this image . . .
has been realized - even recognized?
[p. 1]

      Has the search been successful?
Have I been able to realize the image of
myself and my country that has been
with me since early boyhood? I leave this
for the reader to judge. All I can say --
and all I know is this: I have never . . .
[tried] to build my happiness at the
expense of others. In every decision I
have made, in every action I took, I have
been directed by my firm belief in the
dignity of man and his right to freedom,
to peace, and to equality. I have found
myself in friendship, in love, in work that
helped those around me to live a better
life, in the triumph of truth over
falsehood . . .

      I have never sought power; for
early in my life I discovered that my
strength lies within me -- in my absolute
devotion to what is right, just, and
beautiful. So far, the search has not
ended - nor do I believe that it will ever
end. For with every action we take to
realize ourselves, we fulfill the will of
God, and His will is everlasting. There is
a long way for me and my people to go
before we achieve a life where love,
peace, prosperity and the integrity of
man prevail. May God guide our steps

and those of our fellow men everywhere [pp. 314-315]

With those words this martyr to peace ends his life's story. It is appropriate that we who share these prayers and dreams hear again the blessing of the Prince of Peace: "Blessed are the peacemakers for they shall be called the children of God." Amen.

1981, 7 October Yom Kippur (Day of Atonement).

Lord God for thousands of years communities of worshippers have expressed what every one of us knows -- sin and evil are ever-present companions on life's way. While some persons are more sensitive to their sin all honest men know its power. It doesn't matter whether we call it breaking the commandments, missing the mark, defiance, alienation, estrangement, or self-centeredness sin is a persistent reality of human life.

Every one of us has known the experience of the apostle, "the good that I intend to do I don't do, and the evil that I try to avoid I fall into." Even if we escape the more blatant sins of cruelty, theft, lying, cheating, or murder none of us can claim with a straight face we have always cared for others as much as we care for our own selves. We have not always treated others with the kindness we miss when others have acted harshly against us.

132

We have learned to live with our sin in a world where moral purity is a luxury few can afford.

If we had to bear the full weight of our failures piled one on top of the other we would be crushed. You are a just God holding us responsible for our acts. Forgive us we pray and cleanse us. Take from us the oppressive burden of guilt. Create within us a new heart and a right spirit.

You are a God of mercy treating us far better than we deserve. On this Day of Atonement, this Yom Kippur, blot out our sins, cast them behind your back and remember them no more., we pray. Amen.

1981, 8 October.

Eternal God this has been a long and eventful day. It was a day of expectations and change of schedules made to be remade. It was a day of anticipation overcome by unanticipated experiences. It was a day we would hardly have deliberately designed. Yet it was another day of our life together disclosing to us who we are. In it there was new insight, challenge, and achievement. Many of us went about our tasks unaware of the swift moving currents surging about us. Each of us did well what he is equipped to do. As always there were the personal hurts and sorrows that are never far from us.

*Now we give this day back to You.
While it was not what we had in mind
before it began; it is what we were given
to work with. We have made the best of it.
Thanks be to You, oh Lord. Amen.*

1981, 13 October 206th Navy Birthday.

*Eternal God we celebrate our
birthday today. Not our individual
birthdays or even that special birthday
of our ship, the PELELIU. Rather we
celebrate the birthday of our Navy a
formidable force in war, a potent power
in peace.*

*For over two hundred years men
have accepted the rigors of our nation's
naval service often without adequate pay
or the recognition by their nation which
they rightfully deserved. They often
endured cramped quarters and
unpalatable food. They were often tossed
about in sailing vessels we speak of
romantically but in which few of us
would have signed on for a second tour.
They knew the biting cold, fiercely
blowing wind and burning sun. When
they turned from sail to steam they were
covered with the dirt and grime of coal.*

*So much of what made their lives
a constant hardship has been changed.
But some things haven't changed and we
share their sorrows and their joys. We
share the mystical experience of the sea
so hard to describe to someone who has*

never known it. We share disciplined training in preparation for events we hope never happen. We share sadness at leaving those we love and joy in returning to them again. We share a conviction that no other job would be quite as satisfying as looking forward to new ports and as yet un-sailed seas. And we share their faith that You are our strength, our very present help in time of trouble, our Maker, Defender, Redeemer, and Friend. Amen.

1981, 14 October.

Eternal God it is time again for the evening prayer. Some of the prayers like some of the days come so naturally. There are events or persons who stand out so prominently that it is easy to praise You for what has been done and the men who have done it. There are other days with special needs which demand our thoughtfulness, our concern and our prayers. There are other times when we have prayed and waited knowing that tattoo would be passed and the time for Evening Prayer was coming ready or not.

It is an awesome experience to pray for the PELELIU. It is awesome because we pray to You the Source and Giver of life. It is awesome because of the expectancy of the men of this ship unlike any other ship we have known. It is awesome because we have come to expect only the best.

Thank You for the homerun prayers that go powerfully over the wall so that we cover all the bases. Thank You for the hits which allow us to get on base and touch the life of some one. It isn't easy to thank You for the pop flys which go up high only to come down without making it possible for someone else to bring us on in. The hardest to thank You for are the strike outs. The issues either curve too fast for us to swing at them or they curve just when we thought we were ready to connect or they catch us off guard. But that's life and that's our prayer tonight. Maybe what we really mean is its great, oh God, to be on a winning team of enthusiastic and professional players, knowing that each one of us contributes something for all of us to be glad about.

Thank You God for the PELELIU team -- this crew and the games well played and the promise and prospect of another time at bat, another day to pray and work together. Amen.

1981, 15 October.

Thank You Lord for quiet times. We are almost afraid to pray such a prayer. Yet it is the quiet times which help us keep our balance and perspective. It is so easy to lose perspective either as individual *men or as a ship's company when the crises or emergencies come thick and fast, just as it is difficult to keep our perspective when we must continually deal with the deviancies and disorders of life.*

We marvel that there are so many men on this ship who live responsible and mature lives and so few whose problems are excuses for irresponsible behavior. As Jesus using the experiences of life about him reminded those who listened, "a little leaven evens out the whole lump". Thank You God for the overwhelming majority of leveling men on the PELELIU whose lives are influences for good, who have such a healthy awareness of who they are that they are able to encourage others simply by being themselves. May the impact of those who have found a satisfying life, not without unanswered questions, be an example to those who are still struggling for a sense of balance and proportion. Accept our thanks for those whose lives shine as lights amidst the confusions and conflicts, the quiet men who appreciate and are renewed by quiet times. Amen.

1981, 20 October.

Gracious God there is rarely a day when we are not aware of the exceptional job someone does. The evening prayer would be far longer if we thanked You for specific individuals or even for divisions or departments who on a given day exemplify that concern for others and determination to succeed which distinguishes this extraordinary crew.

On most ships it would have been the usual and accepted thing for disbursing clerks and data processors to have gotten around to pay adjustments some time before the next pay day. Instead at personal sacrifice and an evident desire to positively contribute to the morale and well-being of their shipmates these men demonstrated again that professional performance which characterizes PELELIU sailors.

And those engineers, God, what a fantastic lot they are! They combine common sense and uncommon dedication moving us closer toward a successful OPPE. While theirs is the most obvious test there is hardly an area of the ship not facing a crucial examination in the next few weeks.

We pray that as we all continue our preparation we may constantly increase our knowledge and refine our skills. Grant we pray that our enthusiasm may not slacken nor our sense of personal responsibility be lessened by our appreciation of the contributions of others.

Undergird us with your strength and power. Instill within us trust and confidence in You so that we may ever be grateful for the work of others. Keep us alert at our watches. Grant us sound and restful sleep to renew us in body and spirit so that we may do all things well. Amen.

1981, 21 October.

Dear God thank You for the men behind the scenes; the night crawlers cheerfully polishing the deck night after night making it almost a holy place, the parachute riggers maintaining survival gear and making other contributions to the protection of life and property, the ship's secretary and his staff pushing papers endlessly meeting administrative demands and deadlines from within and without, the stock clerks and record keepers keeping supplies and equipment flowing, the non-rates and working party members repeatedly moving tons of provisions, the side cleaners washing the ship keeping her presentable and preserved, the boats'n mates and messengers of the watch passing the word, the helmsmen steering our course, the phone talkers and quartermasters, the plotters and spotters charting a safe course, the watches peering into the night, the communicators maintaining contact with a wider world, the

139

corpsmen hearing our complaints and safeguarding our health.

We are like a human body with so many parts. If one part becomes infected or diseased, fractured or impotent the whole body suffers. If the separate parts are strong and well cared for the whole body feels good and works well. Keep the ship's eyes and ears, feet and hands, heart and brain in good health, we pray, so that we may work together in harmony enjoying the benefits of a vital life. Amen.

1981, 22 October.

Dear Lord set us free from the defenses we put up which keep us from understanding ourselves or other persons. Break down the barriers that separate us. Create within us a strong desire to inspire and lead. Make our commitment to truth and integrity our strong armor against hypocrisy and cowardice. Open our eyes to ways we may enhance the dignity and worth of others. Shake us free from the worship of idols which have no power to support and sustain us. Preserve us from being at ease with coercive power which is powerless to win the respect and loyalty of those we lead. Make us more eager to encourage the best in others than to ridicule them for their worst. Help us to realistically examine ourselves to learn whether we expend our energies more for destruction than for constructive growth. Move us a step closer to solutions rather than running headlong into greater problems. Forgive our weaknesses and increase our strengths. Search us and know us and see if there is any right way within and among us. Bless us in all we do that is right and good. Amen.

1981, 2 November.

Dear Lord God what is it that makes some men so trustworthy that we know we can always count on them. Whatever they tell us is the truth. Whatever they do is grounded in a firm conviction that they will do their best in any given situation. Some men are solid, steady, stable. They have problems like everybody else but they never use those problems as excuses for blaming others or defaulting on their responsibilities. There is a quality of life in them which we admire and which contribute to the strength and character of others.

Other men seem to see problems as crises and rarely see deeply enough into themselves or the resources available to them to keep from stumbling over every obstacle.

What are the differences? There is a difference in confidence without which we cannot trust ourselves or anyone else.

There is a difference in acceptance of human characteristics, or capabilities and limitations. There is a difference in that deep down calm which makes for peace.

Long ago your prophet Isaiah said, "They who wait upon the Lord shall renew their strength. They shall mount up with wings like eagles, they shall run and not grow weary, they shall walk and not faint." Let it be so God. Amen.

1981, 3 November.

Another day at sea, oh God! Another day of intense training, hard work, and dedication to improving personnel and material capabilities! So much has been done. So much more crowds in demanding our best efforts. We are grateful to You for the privilege of working with men who refuse to settle for mediocrity or slip-shod performance. It would be easy enough for some men to be content with just getting by, with skating, with gun-decking. But that is not the way of the PELELIU. These are men who have found what so many search for, a challenge for excellence.

We are reminded of the words of a hymn: "Give of your best to the Master, give of the strength of your youth, throw your soul's fresh glowing ardor into the battle for truth."

It is a religious devotion even from many who don't call it such. Even if some of us are frightened by the idea of too easy or too vocal a claim to religious commitment we believe that the strength of youth used for the good of others is an offering to You and a celebration of the privilege of meaningful use of the talents and abilities we have been given.

Grant to us now we pray a restful night safe and secure in your care and keeping. Amen.

1981, 4 November.

Dear Lord God there are so many experiences in a day and every one of them can lead us closer to You. The experiences of disappointment can lead us to reliance on your unfailing love. The experiences of pain can lead us to your comfort. The experiences of shame or guilt can lead us to your forgiveness. The experiences of fear can lead us to trust in your strength. The experiences of sin can lead us to your grace. The experiences of loneliness can lead us to your companionship.

Let your will be done in the experiences of our lives. Let the remembrance of the good things of the past be a bright hope of the happiness of the future. Thank You God for restoring our souls. Amen.

1981, 5 November.

Eternal God we rejoice with those who were recognized today for their outstanding contributions. We listened to the citations which expressed praise and appreciation for accomplishments exceeding the usual expectations of performance and were proud of them and for them. Their distinction brings honor to us all.

There are many lessons we learn from such joyous occasions. Few persons gain honor by seeking it as a goal in itself. It is rather in a fortuitous combination of circumstances that honors come. Not only must men excel in what they do, there must also be those who value their work and recognize and applaud it. As the Bible reminds us, "many are called but few are chosen". Even as we rejoice with our shipmates who know the sweet satisfaction of high acclaim, we feel the disappointment of others whose recognition must wait for another time and place.

As the Apostle Paul admonished, let each of us be pleased with those who rejoice in life's fullness even as we must often times share the sorrow of those who must endure its emptiness. We learn all over again the lesson of Jesus' parable of the talents. While we differ in our abilities, it is the fullest use of what we

144

have that brings the affirmation, "well done good and faithful servant enter into the joy which is yours." Help each of us to do his best and in doing so feel the satisfaction which comes with such efforts. Amen.

1981, 30 November the beginning of Refresher Training (REFTRA).

Eternal God every time we go to sea it is like starting all over again. The things we thought we knew so well have to be learned anew. Old shipmates who had become so much a part of our lives are left behind. Some of them go on to other assignments and new opportunities. Others complete their enlistment and choose to find their place again in civilian society. New men come aboard to begin the process of becoming a part of this crew. For some it is a new chance to leave mistakes behind and to make a new start. It isn't easy for them or for us. So much of our life together revolves around the challenges and accomplishments of the past. There are always the disappointments with our selves or with others which have to be dealt with. Trust has to be reestablished and confidence restored. New lessons have to be learned and old misunderstandings set aside. As we begin this intense period of REFTRA we seek your blessings upon us.

For those who have the responsibilities of leadership we pray the grace to encourage and inspire. For all of us on whom others depend we pray for strength and integrity to perform our assigned tasks so as to bring credit and honor to all of us.

Grant now we pray rest and peace and a commitment to an even better use of our abilities tomorrow than we have made of them today. Amen.

1981, 1 December.

Dear Lord let's make this a short one, o.k.? The anxiety level rises, tempers get shorter, we become more critical of one another. Things don't go right. And that's hard for us on the PELELIU to take because we aren't used to it. We're used to giving our best and being proud of the results. We don't have a doubt but that we will do our best when we're really put to the test. Help us now in our frustration to be still and know that You are God, that You have made us and not we ourselves. In quietness and confidence You will be our strength. We are glad, for we know that we can do all things through Christ who strengthens us. Amen.

1981, 2 December.

Eternal Father each day brings some new opportunity for growth and insight. Sometimes it is through the extraordinary efforts of ordinary men that we see the virtues often hidden in daily performance. Sometimes it is through the spontaneous act of generosity of a more mature person that we get a clearer picture of what it means to be a leader of men. Personal advantage is set aside for the sake of someone else. Sometimes men already tasked with demanding jobs see an opportunity to realistically provide for the needs of others and seize that opportunity without a murmur or complaint.

Greatness of character like other forms of art comes about through dedication and perseverance. It is genuine when it appears spontaneous and inevitable when the effort goes unnoticed because of the naturalness of the effect. Caught-up as we are in the necessity of demands from without, we sometimes forget that true growth comes when the demands evolve from within. Let the demands we make on others be but a reflection of the disciplined demands we make on ourselves. Let our actions speak more eloquently than our words as we work together in this life which we have

147

chosen and for which we have been selected. Amen.

1981, 3 December.

Eternal God night after night we offer prayers of gratitude, prayers that highlight acts of kindness, compassion and concern we have seen our shipmates perform. We use elevated language to lift the human spirit and draw us close to You. We reaffirm the goodness of which we believe each of us is capable. Yet like the Apostle Paul we are painfully aware that the good we say we want to do is not what we always do and the evil we maintain we want to avoid is what we often wind up doing.

We find it hard to accept that normal decent men would deliberately make life harder for themselves and other men. Yet this is too obvious to ignore. Because we have personally done menial labor for insufficient pay we know how thankless it is. Because we have been a plumber's helper and unstopped toilets and sewer lines and cleaned septic tanks we know first-hand what a literally shitty job that is. So tonight we thank You for our HTs and A Gang men who wade through the filth to make our living spaces clean and sanitary.

It is very hard, oh God, to feel kindly toward those among us who have such low self-esteem and such plain disregard for others that they deliberately make messes other people have to clean up. If they don't care about the trouble they cause others how can we hope that they have any sensitivity to prayers or to the goodness of life for which You have created us. Yet tonight we pray that they may have some twinge of conscience so as to turn from their senseless actions.

Create in each of us a clean heart and a right spirit so that we might worship and glorify You by the way we serve one another. Amen.

1981, 7 December.

Eternal God the children of Israel wandered forty years in the wilderness. For forty days Jesus struggled alone in the wilderness. It appears we will steam forty hours in this wilderness of fog. In the wilderness there are always dangers lurking. In the wilderness one is always alone. But the wilderness wandering of the Israelites was but a preparation for their conquest of the Promised Land. And the wilderness waiting of Jesus was but a deepening of commitment to your ways which lay ahead of him.

We too sometimes wander in the wilderness of our personal lives unsure of the way which leads to victory. We too sometimes wait in the wilderness for *some passionate purpose to take hold of us. Protect us from the dangers and preserve us in the struggles of life.*

As we hear the ship's whistle sounding its constant penetrating warning to others may we also hear its comfort to us. Through the wilderness and fog of life may we hear your challenging warnings and the sure and certain hope that we are always in your care and keeping. Amen.

1981, 8 December.

Dear God and Father evening prayers are like meals. Some we come to because we are hungry and we enjoy what is prepared for us. When we have eaten we are satisfied and full. Some we come to simply because it is time to eat again and the meal nourishes us. Some we come to with excited expectations, anticipating the special food and delighting in it. The enjoyment of the meal is not always dependent on the expertise of the cook. Even a simple meal may become a feast and a gourmet feast may sometimes leave us unimpressed. Jesus referred to himself as the bread of life and said those who fed on him would not be hungry.

We all get hungry sometimes. It may be the hunger of loneliness, or of misery, or of guilt unresolved, or of life without purpose or meaning, or of confusion or perplexity. Feed us, oh God, with the bread of life that our spirits may be satisfied. Give us solid, nourishing food that we may be strong and healthy in spirit as in body. And prepare a table before us as the Psalmist long ago said with the abundance of your galley. Make us glad for the everyday food of strength and health and help us to appreciate and enjoy the special delicacies of compassion and satisfaction in work well done. Amen.

1981, 9 December.

Eternal God each of us has a job to do. A vital part of mine is to offer to You these evening prayers on behalf of this extraordinary ship. There are so many different jobs to be done that few of us have any notion of what many of the rest of us are about. Few have the privilege of knowing the big picture.

We are awed by the Commanding Officer on whom the success of the whole venture depends and who can never escape final responsibility for all that takes place here.

We are impressed by the agility of the Executive Officer who is at one and the same time required to be a wise orderer of priorities, a skillful manager, a virtual ringmaster orchestrating an unlimited and overlapping succession of events moving toward established goals.

We marvel at the tenacity of our Department Heads who like adept jugglers keep so many balls in the air conscious that a break in the rhythm means an abrupt halt to the whole show. Strenuous as these demands are they at least are accompanied by a sense of meaning and purpose. We pray for these our respected and seasoned leaders. We pray also for Division Officers, Chief Petty Officers and Petty Officers on whom fall the burden of understanding people and translating plans into performance.

We would not neglect in our prayers that larger company of men whose role at this stage is to take orders not give them, to be obedient and loyal even when their own desires might be in other directions.

Lord God we pray for our ship, the PELELIU, that each of us may give his best for the good of all of us. Grant us rest and peace throughout the night and a sense of calm confidence and dedicated strength equal to tomorrow's opportunities. Amen.

1981, 10 December.

Tonight for our Evening Prayer we turn to the ancient poet of Israel whose words have brought hope and help to persons like us throughout the centuries. Join me now as we pray with the Psalmist:

To Thee, O Lord, I lift up my soul; In Thee I trust. Let me not be ashamed; do not let my enemies triumph over me. Yea, none who wait for Thee shall be ashamed. Show me Thy ways, O Lord; teach me Thy paths. Guide me in Thy truth and instruct me; for Thou art the God of my salvation. For Thee I wait all day. Remember, O Lord, Thy tender mercies and Thy loving kindnesses for they are from everlasting. Remember not the sins of my youth, nor my transgressions. Remember me according to Thy faithfulness for Thy name's sake, O Lord. Amen. [from Psalm 25:1-7]

1981, 14 December.

Eternal God as we complete this evolution and wearily turn in for a night of rest before beginning another arduous day, we offer You our prayers of gratitude for the safety of our crew and their dedicated performance.

Each time we come along side another ship for replenishment we reaffirm the fact of the interdependence of life. No one can go it alone. The ship is but a larger manifestation of our individual lives.

Messages have to be sent and received; we offer our gratitude for those signalmen who from their lofty perch often see the grandeur of your starry heavens and express a more open devotion to You.

As we continue at a safe distance along-side another ship for an extended period of time it takes sharp eyes, steady hands, quick minds and confident experience. So we thank You for the wing walkers and bridge watches. The sturdy muscles and sure hands of riggers and deck hands who make happen the purpose of the rendezvous as we take on fuel to fire the boilers our engineers tend without the advantages and refreshment of seeing the dramatic beauty of it all.

For the special skills of all hands and the purposeful pride in the work on which we all depend we offer our thanks knowing that as You have sustained us in this evolution and throughout the long and tedious tasks of today so You will renew our strength and replenish our spirits for what awaits us tomorrow. Amen. .

1981, 15 December.

Lord God, Heavenly Father, we come to You weary from our work and frustrated by our efforts. Well made plans must constantly be revised by events over which we have little or no control.

We hear the news of the desperate plight of the people of Poland and with sorrowful hearts know that even with courage and skill there is little we can

154

do to alter their course in history. Yet there is for us a strong message in what is happening there. Maybe the rigorous demands of the kind of training we are going through are set in perspective.

We are men who have chosen the profession of arms. We could have chosen other uses for our lives. If we lived in a world where all men valued peace and freedom and the good of his neighbor there would be no need for what we do. But we don't have the luxury of such a world. Rather we live in a world where political processes are often intertwined with military processes.

We thank You that in this Advent season we are not called upon to defend our basic values with military force. Still we are painfully aware that peace is a precarious treasure which men of courage must be willing to safeguard. We dare not see our training as a mere game diverting us from a life of ease or monotony. The lessons we are learning now with stress on body and spirit are the lessons of our profession which cannot be learned in the instant when they must be used.

While we pray for peace to men of goodwill throughout the earth in this Christmas season we pray also for the stamina to persevere in acquiring proficiency in the profession which we perform even with troubled consciences and penitent spirits.

With the poet we pray, "God of Grace and God of Glory on Thy people pour Thy power, bring Thy bud to glorious flower. Grant us wisdom, grant us courage for the facing of this hour." [Harry Emerson Fosdick] *Amen.*

1981, 16 December.

It was suggested that the prayer tonight might simply be, "God help us." So it is.

God help us to appreciate the special skills of the FTG observers whose purpose is to help us become even better than we are.

God help us not merely to get through this ordeal but to do so with a heightened sense of pride and satisfaction.

God help us to draw deeply from the strength which comes from You and our reliance on one another.

God help us to keep both a sense of perspective and a sense of humor.

God help us through this night and the days and nights to come to be glad to be a part of this extraordinary ship.

God help us to be alert at our watches and restful in our sleep. Amen.

1981, 17 December   last night at sea before holiday stand-down.

Dear God and Father this is the last night of our prayers at sea before Christmas and the New Year. It is a time of reflection and anticipation. We wish our shipmates and friends who make no profession of faith the joys of the season, joys of family and good times. We wish our Jewish shipmates and friends a Happy Hanukkah remembering with them an event centuries ago when by your miraculous grace a light shown in the darkness as a vigil of the eternal light of freedom and deliverance. We wish our Christian shipmates and friends a Merry Christmas in which we celebrate the most significant event in our western heritage. The birth of Jesus was the dividing line of time making its imprint on all who lived in its light or shadow. The miracle of the divine in the very midst of the human gathered about it the simplest and most humble experiences of ordinary men -- shepherds who heard angelic voices proclaiming, "Glory to God in the highest and peace to men of goodwill on earth". Even as it gathered about it the most elegant and elaborate gifts of bright shining stars and wise men bearing gifts more significant in their symbolism than in their price.

157

As we reflect on the year fast passing we remember persons who inconspicuously touched our lives in ways long to be remembered and events which shaped our destiny.

As we anticipate the New Year soon to open before us we look forward to new and exotic places, to extraordinary events which lend richness and flavor to our ordinary lives. We pray for one another: love, joy, and peace; light for our darkness and hope for our days. Let heaven and nature sing of joy to the world for the Lord has come. Amen.

1982, 4 January   first night at sea after holiday stand-down.

Eternal God once again at sea we are grateful for the joys of the Christmas season just passed. The illusive dream of peace was rekindled as we heard once more the familiar story of your love for mankind in the Prince of Peace. For centuries men have called You mighty Counselor as they have sought comfort in your counsel of compassion. Quickly the celebration of Jesus' birth gave way to the opening of a New Year. We reflected seriously on the demanding year left behind as we turned with anticipation toward the challenging year being born. And as is often the case with us some of our shipmates and friends made their

158

departures while new and anxious shipmates have taken their places beside us.

May this be a time for renewed dedication. May the bright promises of the year ahead be for us a guiding star to steer our course, a destiny we receive and achieve as co-creators with You and with one another. May all that we are and all that we hope to become be solidly anchored in faith in your eternal goodness, your ever present strength, and in our purest devotion to the best use of our highest aspirations. Amen.

1982, 5 January.

Oh God sometimes we try so hard to imagine what someone else is thinking or feeling, to hurt where he hurts, to know what he is afraid of or what motivates him. Sometimes we don't try very hard at all because we are aware we can really know someone only if he lets us. You have made us this way. That is the joy and burden of personal freedom. That freedom is not only a gift from You it is the very reflection of your nature. We can only know You because You have chosen to let us know You.

The Apostle Paul said it long ago as he talked about what it means to be a human being. Our knowledge is always imperfect in this life. We only know bits and pieces of persons and it is so

159

frustrating because we live in an age when we know so much about so many impersonal things. But people are not machines not even highly sophisticated computerized machines.

People are, well, people! And people plan and dream and hope and hurt and try and fail and succeed. People are vulnerable. Some times because we are afraid that others won't like us or understand us or accept us we keep our distance. We look forward to the time when our imperfect knowledge and understanding will be whole and complete. We look forward to a time when we shall know even as we have been known, to a time when we shall understand even as we have been understood.

As a very wise and great man once prayed, "O Divine Master grant that I may not so much seek to be understood as to understand; to be loved as to love; for it is in giving that we receive; it is in pardoning that we are pardoned." [St. Augustine]

Help us God to take confidence in the faith that You know us and understand us and love us now and always. Amen.

1982, 6 January.

Eternal God how we marvel at the strength, endurance and spirit of this crew! They seem to thrive on difficult tasks. They prove over and over again that a positive spirit is contagious. They sweat and strain using their muscles and brains exuberantly and enthusiastically. They can be counted on to give their best simply because that is what's expected of them. They have found a secret some people spend all their lives looking for -- if you do whatever you have to do with determination, with dedication to doing it to the best of your ability it brings lasting satisfaction. Why are the men of the PELELIU this way?

We can find a lot of reasons but even all of these cannot fully answer our question. So it seems God only knows. Maybe that's it. You know who we are and have given us the privilege of working with one another in ways that make us better men.

Now as we stop for a little while from our labors give us a restful night, renew our strength and give us confidence in your grace which is always sufficient for our needs. Amen.

1982, 7 January.

Eternal God religion is the strangest, most mysterious force in the universe. Under the power of their religious convictions men have murdered, pillaged, raped, and committed the grossest tortures. Wars have been fought and people slaughtered

161

under the conviction that the world is a corrupt and evil place and the chosen ones have been singled out to purify it by getting rid of those who differ from them. Is it any wonder that some men want nothing to do with any form of religion? Even that faith which proclaims its allegiance to the Prince of Peace has not been immune to divisiveness which sows seeds of destruction.

Especially in times of great social upheaval when old values seem ineffective, when there is little certainty, when the changes are too swift and shattering to be assimilated men have often singled out a particular belief such as their own particular belief in the Bible as the only certainty in a chaotic world.

Simply because it is so mysterious, because men have deep within them a conviction that creation is better than destruction that love must triumph over hate, that brotherhood is necessary for survival men have held onto a feeling that deep within man is the yearning for a kingdom or realm not of this world. This ship is not that kingdom nor is that realm of human brotherhood identifiable with any human organization, institution, or society.

Men are often torn apart by the conflict between their inabilities to live *in time with their hearts set on eternity. Men have often retreated from the world to take sanctuary either in monasteries or made their particular religious community a citadel against all others accepting them only if they renounce everything else to live with them in their fortress.*

Let us never forget that walls erected to keep people out also make prisoners of those who must live within. Yet You chose to come into such a world and live as one of us setting us free from fears either of death or hell giving those who would accept it a new heart and a new spirit, a spirit of love, joy, peace, patience, and compassion. Even if we are sickened by the abuse of religious faith we dare not abandon a vital faith which sustains us. We pray tonight as men have always prayed. "Create within us a new heart and renew a right spirit within us." Amen.

1982, 13 January.

This is the Ship's Chaplain. It is a time honored custom for ships of our Navy to have Evening Prayers just before taps. These are offered by the Ship's Chaplain or other Chaplains when they are embarked. Before tonight's prayer let me invite you to celebrate Roman Catholic Mass with us tomorrow morning at 0630 or Protestant Morning Prayers at 0700. Both are held in the

Ship's Library on the 3rd deck. Now would you quietly and reverently pause for the Evening Prayer.

Eternal God for months the men of the PELELIU have worked together with rare enthusiasm and encouraging pride. On every occasion which has demanded their best they have given it. Even high expectations have often been exceeded. When lesser men would have grumbled or complained at the unanticipated they have shown themselves men of remarkable dedication. An even greater challenge now confronts us. It is not the challenge of performing our primary mission for we are confident that will be faithfully done nor is it the challenge of long hours and flexible schedules. It is rather the challenge of maintaining this ship's unique spirit, a spirit of cooperation and courtesy, of hospitality and hope, and of confidence and perseverance. We have come to know and respect one another as we have worked and trained together. Now greater numbers of men must live and work together at every level of operation. Now, Sailors and Marines, Staff and Ship's Company, Aviators and many types of specialists must practice the highest values of mature manhood living in comfortable but crowded spaces, utilizing facilities maximally and wisely and judiciously using always limited time.

Tonight we have moved into a new phase of our existence. The time of preparation lies behind us. The time of proof has opened before us.

So, oh God, we pray for patience and fortitude, for peace through power, and for brotherliness in common commitment. Refresh and renew us so that we may now and always be men of good humor, of compassion and consideration who gratefully accept your strength as sufficient for every opportunity. Bless and keep us always in your care. Amen.

1982, 17 January.

Eternal God today was a Sunday like none we have known before on the PELELIU. It began early with expectation and excitement. It closes now with admiration and satisfaction. While what we did was an exercise it was not merely an exercise. It was an affirmation that this extraordinary company of men can and will be ready when called upon to provide relief and protection, care and comfort for those whose lives may someday depend on the r use of the skills so admirably displayed today. We are proud of the humanitarian mission of this ship and even prouder of the exemplary spirit in *which that mission has been demonstrated in practice as a promise of performance whenever and wherever the need may arise.*

Underneath our lives are your everlasting arms and your strength is the source of our strength.

The cooperation and joint effort today came from men who though they wear different uniforms and insignia belong to a single humanity created in your image and likeness.

Grant now we pray a well-earned restful night to those who may sleep and to watch-standers alertness and peace. Amen.

1982, 20 January.

Men as we pray tonight we are very much conscious of the effect of the weather on our combined operation. We realize how fortunate we were today that no life was lost or that anyone was severely injured. We are mindful of those men on the beach tonight in the cold rain. We are aware of the dangers or perils which we must often face with courage. So tonight I ask you to prayerfully share with me these three verses of the Navy Hymn which most directly apply to us. Let us pray:

Eternal Father strong to save whose arm hath bound the restless wave

Who biddst the mighty ocean deep its own appointed limits keep.

Oh hear us as we cry to Thee for those in peril on the sea.

Lord guard and guide the men who fly through the great spaces in the sky.

Be with them always in the air in darkening storms or sunlight fair.

Oh hear us as we lift our prayer for those in peril in the air.

Eternal Father grant we pray to all Marines both night and day,

The courage, honor, strength, and skill their land to serve, thy law fulfill.

Be Thou our shield forevermore from every peril to the Corps.

Lord hear our prayer. Amen.

1982, 21 January.

Lord God long ago a prophet in Israel asked what You expect of men. He wondered if sacrifice and burnt offerings were necessary. He wanted to be sure he understood what You require of men. The answer was startlingly simple. It was that men should practice justice, show kindness, and walk with integrity before You.

Oh God justice was the fair use of what each one had for the good of everyone. It was when each part was well tuned to the smooth working of the whole. This strenuous period has been a time of justice. We offer You our thanks. Kindness has been the rule rather than the exception. Kindness is believing that people are capable of doing what is expected of them and want to contribute to the best of their abilities. This has been a period of kindness when much was expected of each man and each man met the challenge of high expectations. Walking with integrity before You means thinking neither too little nor too much of ourselves. It is pride which avoids arrogance and determination without ruthlessness. It has been a period of integrity.

We are pleased and proud. We are not so foolish as to imagine that any one of us is sufficient by himself to meet life's opportunities. We started out together in the PELELIU as men who affirmed that we would faithfully perform every mission assigned to us by the power of your strength working in us and through us for peace. We have kept the faith. This we offer back to You with grateful hearts tonight for your even greater faithfulness as we joyously count the hours until our return home. Amen.

1982, 8 February.

Eternal God we have come here often in our life together on the PELELIU. There is power and peace in prayer. We have shared good times and the satisfaction of work well done and have thanked You for those special meanings. We have asked for forgiveness and acceptance and understanding even as we have marveled at the enthusiastic dedication of our shipmates. Once again we seek your strength and help not to save us from ourselves but to enable us to use the resources we have been given to meet the challenges which we now face in this week of PHIBREFTRA.

Tonight we pray for two of our shipmates and their families. Both are in your care and keeping. One family knows the agonizing sorrow of death -- senseless and shocking. One family knows the agonizing struggle of life - confusing and confounding. Both will inevitably ask why? And neither will find a fully satisfying answer. Yet while there is no complete answer to the question there is a companion in the questioning. Comfort those who feel the deep sorrow of death, restore those who feel the nagging sorrow of life.

As you place your everlasting arms beneath us to give us strength so put your ever loving arms around us to give us courage. May the power of your presence be our confidence and our hope in life and in death. Amen.

1982, 9 February.

Dear God a long time ago a story was told of a man named Sisyphus who rolled a large stone up a hill. Each time he got it almost to the top he slipped and fell and the stone rolled faster and faster to the bottom again. Wearily he picked himself up trudged down the hillside put his strength to the stone and rolled it up once more. That is one way of looking at life. Every time we think we are almost over the top we have to do it all over again. All men get tired of rolling the stone up the hill of life. Weak men give up convinced that it really doesn't matter how hard you try you are never gonna make it anyway. Men of faith start over again as often as necessary. Maybe life is not so much an unending series of accomplishments as it is a process of putting our strength into each day's task and doing the best we can.

Jesus said to men rolling the stone up life's hill, "Don't be anxious about tomorrow. You've got enough to worry about in every day's responsibilities." Wise men learn that we only get one day at a time. They know that the best preparation for a satisfying tomorrow is to do today whatever has to be done to the best of their abilities. We may not always make it to the top but please help us Lord to at least use whatever resources we each have to keep on keeping on. Amen.

1982, 10 February.

For our evening prayer tonight we turn to the words of a magnificent hymn. May the words express our own true prayer and confident faith:

O God our help in ages past, our hope for years to come,

Our shelter from the stormy blast and our eternal home.

A thousand ages in Thy sight are like an evening gone,

Short as the watch that ends the night before the rising sun.

Time like an ever-rolling stream bears all its sons away.

They fly forgotten as a dream dies at the opening day.

Our God our help in ages past, our hope for years to come;

Be Thou our guard while life shall last and our eternal home. Amen.

1982, 11 February.

Eternal God we thank You tonight for the beautiful weather today. It was a gloriously bright day. We were a bit concerned last night that it might not turn out so fine. There is always greater danger and disappointment when the weather is bad. We have been fortunate on the PELELIU. Safety is a reflection of our attitudes about ourselves and other people.

Accidents rarely just happen. They usually result from carelessness and carelessness is just what it says, "I could care less about what happens to me or to you." Men who care about themselves care about other people. Even when the weather makes carefulness all the more essential as it did in Kernel Egress and Kernel Usher these remarkable men of the PELELIU showed they cared enough to watch out for one another.

We will arise very early in a few short hours for another test of our abilities and our caring. Give us restful though short sleep. Let us awake alert and ready to care enough to make it a good day. Even if we can't be cheerful so early in the day help us to be attentive to what we do.

Every day is a gift from You to us to be used and given back to You at night. Accept our thanks for the privilege of caring for one another knowing that we care because You care for us now and always. Amen.

1982, 22 February.

Oh God as deployment gets closer we find ourselves changing. There is a sense of urgency about what we do and a *conviction that it is essential for our readiness and safety. We see mounting frustration in our actions and hear it in our speech.*

Long ago a very wise man said, "As a man thinks in his heart so is he." [Proverbs 23:7]

Language is the way other people see into our minds and sense those things about which we feel deeply. Clear speech comes from clear minds. Foul speech pollutes the atmosphere of human interaction. It degrades those against whom it is used and dehumanizes those who resort to it. Forgive us for language which profanes the sacredness of life. "Let the words of our mouths and the thoughts of our hearts be acceptable in your sight, oh Lord our strength and our redeemer." [Psalm 19:14] *Amen.*

1982, 23 February.
Men, tomorrow is Ash Wednesday the beginning of Lent the period of preparation leading up to Easter. All around the world Christians will be gathering for prayer and meditation. We invite you to Ash Wednesday service at 1130 in the Ship's Library. We urge all Christians to participate. Let us pray:

Eternal God, life is a rhythm of laughter and tears, of successes and failures, of triumphs and disappointments. Mardi Gras is followed by Ash

Wednesday. Revelry brings on reverie. Life isn't always fun but it isn't always sadness either. The dark night of the soul often leads to the bright dawn of the spirit.

When we are young we are impatient with life because we are trapped in the present. We find it hard to believe that it is ever gonna be any different than it is right now. We are like men who pray Lord give me patience and give it to me right now! Help us to appreciate the rhythms of life -- its ups and downs as constant as the motion of the ocean. How boring it would be if it were always the same. Keep us from going under when we're down or floating away when we're up. Help us to know that You are the constancy amidst the change, our peace and our joy. Amen.

1982, 24 February   Ash Wednesday.

Dear God we are thankful that there is a time for prayer in our life together on the PELELIU. Our prayers are expressions of faith in You and gratitude for your gifts to us. There are times when our need is also for recognition of our sins, of our distance from You and from one another, of the lack of wholeness when we seem to be coming apart at the seams. On this Ash Wednesday we hear again the words of Scripture: "If we say we have no sin we deceive ourselves and the truth is not in us; but if we confess our sins God is faithful and just to forgive us our sins and to cleanse us from all unrighteousness." [I John 1:8]

Therefore we humbly confess our sins unto You Almighty and Merciful Father. We have erred and strayed from your ways. We have followed too often the devices and desires of our own hearts. We have offended against your holy will. We have not done things which we should have done and have done things which we should not have done. Have mercy upon us, O Lord.

Strengthen those who confess their faults. Restore those who earnestly desire forgiveness according to your promises declared to all mankind in Christ Jesus our Lord. And grant, O Most Merciful Father, for his sake that we may from now on live a godly, righteous, and faithful life to the glory of your holy name. May You in your loving kindness grant to each of us forgiveness for his sins and power to accept your forgive - ness. Redirect our lives by the grace, comfort, and presence of your Holy Spirit now and evermore. Amen.

1982, 25 February.

Gee God did it have to happen this way? We've really been turning and burning to get everything done on time.

It looks like it's one push after another. What gets us is the feeling of helplessness. Sometimes when we do all we can to make it go right even that isn't good enough. It is so aggravating when planes can't fly or helos can't go up, or there is no assistance when we need it.

But wait a minute. Sure we're disappointed because every day with those we love is so precious to us now in the count-down before deployment. Disappointment is nothing compared to the guilt and remorse we would feel if someone were seriously injured or killed because we didn't give extra effort or take necessary precautions, or meet required qualifications. We're glad You understand that we're disappointed. And care about how we feel. It is good that You won't let us down even when we're feeling down.

Somehow let the word get to our loved ones so that they won't worry. Help us to trust You to care for them and for us. Amen.

1982, 26 February.

God what a beautiful and awesome sound is the whosh of those harriers. They are powerful machines piloted by gutsy men. There are lessons here that ennoble the spirit.

What an incredible act of faith it is every time one of those planes

176

accelerates off the flight deck and is airborne and then like a hummingbird it hovers for its descent. What courage is required in leaving the solidly familiar for the dark waiting open-ness. What trust is essential when one man's life is in the hands of other men on whose skill and dedication he must rely. In them we see again that there is no solitary achievement in human life only one man's glory brought about by other men's unrecognized contributions.

Let the lessons of the harriers help us get off the ground of the commonplace by committing ourselves to a soaring faith, courage, and trust set free by a mature responsibility for and with one another. So help us God. Amen.

1982, 27 February.

Before the Evening Prayer, let me encourage you to worship tomorrow at a church in the community. Roman Catholic Mass will be celebrated at 0900 at the Naval Station Chapel which is only a short walk from Pier 6. Protestant worship is held there at 1030. Protestant worship is also held at the Galilee Navy Family Chapel at Cabrillo Housing at 1100. For those of you who have duty or wish to worship on board we plan to have Christian worship in the Ship's Library at 0800. Now let us pray:

Eternal God we thank You and praise You for the safe and successful completion of this mission. As we have done so often before, again we marvel at the spirit of this crew. We believe such an extraordinary spirit is more than our achievement. You have blessed our human spirits by the gift of your divine spirit of peace and power. We thank You also for your watchful care of our families. Give us now a restful night so that whatever we do tomorrow will restore and re-create us in thankfulness to You. Amen.

1982, 15 March.

Eternal God the seas have been a bit rougher today. For some both new men aboard and others not so new it was not a pleasant experience. As is often the case we found that we had to be flexible. Even well-made plans had to be changed and a replenishment scheduled for tomorrow was done tonight. As we watched the smaller ship starboard of the KAWISHIWI rise up out of the water like some great sea creature we uttered a prayer of gratitude for this magnificent ship. But the greater magnificence was more eloquently expressed by one of the phone talkers who said, "Chaplain isn't it wonderful how so many men work together." It is wonderful, oh God. May we never lose the ability to be full of wonder at the spirit of common purpose and dedication with which You have blessed this ship. Amen.

1982, 16 March.

Dear Lord God for some of us each new day brings new events and challenges. For some of us the work of today is very much the same as that of yesterday. Some of us thrive on change and challenge. Some of us find satisfaction in the security of the familiar. Some of us are required to do work for a period of time such as mess cooking or night crawling or compartment cleaning which we would not choose to do very long if we had a choice. Most of the men who do this work do it with the dedication of men who realize its importance even if it is not praised very highly or very often. We are grateful for these men and the work they do.

If we tend to think that we have work to do which is beneath us help us to remember there is more smallness in the way we do our work than in the job itself. Some men have learned a secret which makes whatever they do important. They do it for your glory and the benefit of others and that somehow makes it worthwhile. Help us to practice your presence in whatever we do so that we may experience your peace and your *power in this present moment and in all the unknown days to come.*

Renew and refresh us by your divine spirit so that we may encourage one another by a cheerful and positive human spirit. Amen.

1982, 27 March departure from Long Beach, CA on the PELELIU's first WESTPAC.

Before the Evening Prayer, let me invite you to share in the religious services tomorrow. Senior Chief Long will begin a Sunday School Class at 0830 which is to continue throughout the deployment. At 0930 the Ship's Chaplain will have Protestant Worship. We are pleased that Father Kane who has provided us such outstanding Catholic coverage for almost two years will be celebrating Roman Catholic Mass at 1030. Master Chief Tindall will be leading the Mormon or LDS Service at 11:30. Tomorrow evening at 2100 we will have a Christian Song Service. All religious services are being held in the Ship's Library/Chapel Area on the third deck. See you there. Now please join me for the Evening Prayer.

Eternal God there are days and events we prepare for with such intensity and enthusiasm that when they arrive they are almost anticlimactic. There are also days and events which arrive as a fulfillment of promise and hope. We have known such a day today. Our WESTPAC has begun.

As You have blessed us thus far on our way we know we can count on your continued care. Accept our thanks for the strength and stamina which has brought us to this hour. Let the reputation we enjoy become even more renowned. May the bonds of respect and admiration between us grow as we share new and exciting experiences. Let the power of your peace be our hope and our help in this the PELELIU's greatest venture. Amen.

1982, 29 March en-route from Long Beach, CA to Honolulu, Hawaii.

Eternal God each day moves us deeper into our WESTPAC Deployment. It strikes us now that our lives are the big deployment. We set out from the port of birth with whatever equipment we have received from our parents and our parents' parents. We sail through fair weather and foul. We either do personal PMS making alterations and improvements getting our PQS checked off, or we begin to stagnate, degenerate or malfunction when the going gets rough. We experience the excitement of strange ports along the way which deeply affects the way we see ourselves and the rest of the world.

We plan and execute and revise and adjust and change course when necessary. All the while You are our Skipper who never leaves the bridge when there is a hint of danger. You are always near aware of whatever affects our course. What a paradigm of life this is!

As we as Sailors hold our Captain in awe and obey his commands so we as men stand ever in awe of You on whom our life's ship of destiny depends. As sailors we are obedient to him who carries the responsibility for all the crew. As men may we be obedient to You whose crew is all human kind. As we pray for a safe and successful WESTPAC Deployment, we pray even more for a fitting and faithful voyage on the big deployment of life. At the end may we hear the shouts of joy which welcome us home to You forevermore. Amen.

1982, 31 March.

Dear Lord God when Jesus began his ministry he turned to the words of the prophet Isaiah. He affirmed that he had come to preach good news to the poor, to release the captives, to restore sight to the blind, to lighten the bondage of the oppressed, and to proclaim your favor to all. Sometimes we are poor in spirit because we have spent all we had of faith and trust. Sometimes we are blind to our own needs and to the hurts and *longings of others. Sometimes we are oppressed by our inability to cope with our situation. Even worse, sometimes we are unaware that You are a very present help in time of trouble, our sure and strong defense, our companion and our peace. Whatever our need You are always more ready to answer than we are to ask. Set us free to be what we were created to become -- sons of the Living God. Forgive our sins, remove our guilt, restore our faith by the power at work within us to know and to do your will. Amen.*

1982, 12 April   RIMPAC '82 off Hawaii.

Eternal God what an assembly of people there is on the PELELIU for RIMPAC. It is an awesome concentration of ability and power. As the number of persons grows so grows the challenge and opportunity of living harmoniously together. The sheer acts of communicating and coordinating require additional perseverance and patience. To feed and house so diverse a group is no small task. Making the various activities fit together so that everything goes according to plan is no easy matter.

We are but one unit in a gigantic operation. Such displays of strength are still essential deterrents to evil and elements of the pursuit of peace in a world not yet rid of aggression and forceful dominance. As we are men equipped and trained for war who know the terrors of destruction we are also men who value peace to such an extent that we assume the burden of moral guilt to maintain it.

Protect us from the dangers of carelessness or cowardice. Keep us safe in the responsible performance of our duties. Preserve us always in dedication to freedom and honor and human dignity. Strengthen us, we pray, for the tasks at hand and for our dependence on one another. Amen.

1982, 17 April.

Men before we offer the Evening Prayer let me invite you to worship and study with us tomorrow. At 0830 Senior Chief Long , recent winner of the Navy League's Claude V. Rickett's Award for inspirational leadership, will teach a Bible Study class. At 0930 Chaplain White will preach and Chaplain Stith will sing as part of the Protestant worship. At 1030 Father Dansak who is to helo over from USS MOBILE will celebrate Roman Catholic Mass. He will hear confessions at 1015, At 1130 Master Chief Tindall will lead the Mormon or LDS Service. All services will be in the Ship's Library/Chapel on the third deck. Now let us pray:

Father God accept whatever good there has been in this day and forgive whatever evil there might have been.

Give us a sense of anticipation for tomorrow so that our days may not run monotonously into one another. Help each of us to find something appropriate to re-create, renew and refresh him. Amen.

1982, 22 April   continuing on WESTPAC after leaving Hawaii.

Eternal God today we set sail again. As always there was both joy and sadness. Increasingly we say goodby to shipmates who have been with us through memorable experiences and welcome new men who have come to assume their responsibilities though not to take their places. Human life is such a unique thing. No two of us are the same yet all of us are so much alike. Each one of us has some special quality that sets him apart yet all of us share the same needs for acceptance and recognition, accomplishment and satisfaction. Our lives are like our days. Each one of us has something that sets him apart even while each day is made up of the same number of seconds, minutes and hours.

Keep us open to appreciation of each person's distinctiveness even as we engage in operations or exercises which require our becoming part of something larger than ourselves. We thank You, oh God, that You have chosen to make us so

185

much alike but with such interesting differences. Amen.

1982, 24 April.

Men several of you have expressed an interest in Bible study. If you are really serious about studying the Bible with a very competent teacher then we will see you at 0830 tomorrow for Sunday School. Protestant Worship is at 0930. The Lay Eucharistic Minister will conduct the Roman Catholic service at 1030 and Mormon Services will be at 1130. All these services are to be held in the Ship's Library/Chapel on the third deck. Those of you who are members of the electronic church you will have ample opportunity to worship and learn with the programs scheduled on CCTV. Now let us pray:

Eternal God every day teaches us something about ourselves and others. We have opportunity to see more clearly our strengths and weaknesses. May the lessons we learn teach us even more about You for You are the source of wisdom, our comfort and help in time of trouble, and the strength and hope of our life now and evermore. Amen.

1982, 25 April.

Thank God for picnic makers, music makers, fun makers; For church goers, hymn singers, pray-ers; For spill cleaners, ship drivers, watch standers:

For library keepers, machine fillers, friendly faces; For all who made this a good day. Amen.

After this prayer Cap'n sent me a note saying, "Chaps, that was a chip shot." It was one of my shortest prayers on the PELELIU.

1982, 28 April   after crossing the International Date Line.

Eternal God today we moved from yesterday to tomorrow but it was still today. Twenty-four hours were eclipsed as if they didn't exist. Time is the persistence of memory and the insistence of hope. It is the flow of our common human experiences into our destiny. In the midst of the change and uncertainty of time we seek the permanence and surety of eternity. Time is the crucible in which the solutions of our lives are ground out and refined.

Help us in faith to hear again the words of the poet [Isaac Watts] *and grow in awareness of your eternal care:*

Time like an ever-rolling stream bears all its sons away;

They fly forgotten as a dream dies at the opening day.

O God our help in ages past, our hope for years to come,

Remain our guard while life shall last, and our eternal home. Amen.

1982, 29 April.

Eternal God each day is an opportunity to share someone else's life. Every one of us carries within himself things he wants to share with someone but often for fear they might not understand or accept him if they did understand he is hesitant to open up to another. Some men talk freely and easily but often with little depth or insight. Others wait for an occasion to pour out themselves like a river reaching flood stage.

Today we have listened to men talk of failure as they sought strength and resources to live a life free of addiction. We have felt the disappointment of others for whom well intentioned acts brought only misinterpretation and ridicule. We have heard men speak tenderly and tearfully of a yet unhealed wound of their father's death or their mother's anguish. We have listened and wondered as men spoke almost as if in a vision of reaching for higher states of consciousness in religious or chemical experimentation. Our own memories were revived as men spoke anxiously of their sick children far away and of awareness of their helpless- ness. We heard much more.

We have seen so much compassion and kindness. Yes, we have also seen other dimensions of life -- rudeness and crudeness of word or act, inconsiderateness and bravado attempting to guard against anyone getting close enough to really know them.

The things we have seen and heard cause us to thank You for the gentle-men among us. It is a privilege to be a chaplain here, to have the awesome opportunity to be a symbol of your love and care, a visible and daily reminder that all human life is your gift, a creative possibility moving toward maturity. Thank You for those who wear no sign but whose lives are expressions of that care of brother for brother because You are one Father. Amen.

1982, 1 May.

Before the evening prayer, let me invite you to share in worship and Christian education tomorrow. We are pleased to have Father Hendricks, the 31st MAU Chaplain with us. He will celebrate two Roman Catholic masses -- one at 0800 and the other at 1030. Our Protestant service at 0930 is a special anniversary of the commissioning of USS PELELIU. The Captain will share with us celebrating God's goodness to us. The Mormon Service is at 1130. The Sunday School Class taught by Senior Chief Long has been moved to 1130 in the Crews' Lounge. Many of you will be participating in the Iwo Jima 5K run. We wish you well whether in the success of winning or the simple joy of running. Now let us pray:

Lord God why is it that our ideals are much greater than our achieve - ments? We are too quick to judge, too caustic with our criticism and too eager to challenge what others do and say. We marvel at the superhuman effort of many performing to the best of their ability. Forgive us when we put one another down rather than lift one another up. Help us to believe in the good faith of others until there is sufficient evidence to the contrary. Since You don't give up on us God help us not to give up on ourselves and one another in our efforts to work together for what is best. Amen.

1982, 2 May night before the Second Anniversary of the Commissioning of USS PELELIU.

Though many among us, both Sailors and Marines, were not privileged to experience the dramatic commissioning of USS PELELIU all of us are now part of her life. So join me now in the anniversary prayer:

Dear Lord we thank You for the shared experiences which have given a distinct character and personality to this ship. For the exceptional leadership and human concern which has blessed our life together; for safety in all our operations and your continued protection; for a prevalent spirit of concern and encouragement and the ability of men of widely varying backgrounds, temperaments and interests to live in harmony with one another. For satisfaction that has come from successful accomplishment of every assigned task and wholesome pride which this has engendered.

On this the second anniversary of the commissioning of the PELELIU we rejoice in a brief but glorious past. We thank You for the strength and determination to meet the challenges of the present. We seek renewed devotion and faithfulness to You and to one another in the approaching future. Amen.

1982, 4 May off Iwo Jima.

Eternal God today we stood off the shores of Iwo Jima. Tomorrow many men will go there. We thank You that they are not called upon to go under the terrible barrage their fathers knew a generation ago. It looks so calm and serene that it is hard to imagine the horror of that bloody bit of sand and rock. It is even harder to imagine the thousands of mothers on both sides half-way round the world from one another whose hearts broke with the news, "I regret to inform

191

you that your son died in the service of his country at Iwo Jima."

This was but one of the many cauldrons of death that bring back such memories: places like Guadalcanal, Bougainville, Tarawa, Saipan, Okinawa, and Peleliu where Marines and Sailors gave the last thing they had to give -- their lives -- because they loved home and country more than life itself. Make holy the memories of such places not because we glorify war, but because we strive for peace. Amen.

1982, 6 May.

Thank You Lord for good news! There is enough bad news to go around . Hardly a day passes which does not bring us sadness: news of families in need or crises at home or of serious illness and death. But there is also hardly a day which does not bring us good news of the birth of a baby which brings such joy to the proud father and his shipmates. In the midst of the avalanche of operational messages there are still birthday greetings and happy anniversary wishes.

Mail is such an eagerly awaited event, an incredible boost to morale. A special thanks to the postal clerks who sort it and process it for us.

As You have placed within us sensitive consciences to our human *frailties, so You have also placed within us the necessity of sharing good news with one another.*

Beneath it all is the good news that You love us. You chose to come and live among us as one of us so that we might live with You forever. Because we have heard such good news and believe it let our daily lives express gratitude and joy in the spirit of the Christ we pray. Amen.

1982, 8 May.

Men tomorrow is Mothers Day. We invite you to honor your mother by attending worship. Two Roman Catholic Masses will be celebrated by Father Hendricks – one at 0730 and the other at 1030. Chaplain Uhlemeyer will preach at Protestant worship at 0930. Sunday School Bible Study will be taught by Senior Chief Long at 1030 and Master Chief Tindall will lead the Mormon Service at 1130. All services will be held in the Ship's Library/Chapel on the third deck. Now let us pray:

God they are listening. Every time we offer a prayer of thanks for one group of men others say, "why didn't you mention us too?" We're glad that even if we can't lift up before You in a special way every group of men who contribute to the life of this ship You support them with your grace and strength to do their job in an outstanding manner that benefits us all. Let each of us have the satisfaction within ourselves of knowing there are those who care. Help us to take every opportunity to encourage one another in doing our best.

Long ago Jesus said the real test of Christian commitment was not who said his name the loudest but who did his work for the good of others who needed it. In his spirit of devotion to You we pray. Amen.

1982, 26 May after leaving Subic Bay in the Philippines.

God there are some days which get off to a bad start and go downhill from there. Scheduled events turn into unscheduled delays. Even the weather doesn't cooperate. It is days like these that reinforce the cynical maxim of military life -- hurry up and wait. Oh well, we are at sea again and many of us are glad.

Each day brings us closer to those we love. Each day takes many of us nearer to places we have never been. As we look forward to the new help us to also cherish the familiar. Grant us the power to appreciate both old and new whether of people or places as expressions of the rich diversity of your creation. Amen.

194

1982, 29 May en-route to Pattaya Beach, Thailand from the Philippines. Picked up 62 boat people in the South China Sea.

Eternal God there are days that shine so brilliantly that their radiance lasts a life time. How fitting that on the eve of Pentecost there has been once again a generous outpouring of your Holy Spirit giving new life to your people. What tenderness and compassion has been shown by men who love their own families so much that it is inconceivable that they could do anything but give their best to alleviate suffering or welcome the homeless.

We have seen the truth of Jesus' affirmation, "whatever you have done to the least of these my brethren you have done to me." Accept our gratitude, oh God, for the privilege of caring for others and receiving from them their inexpressible joy.

Out of what would probably have been a sure and certain death for them You have made us a means of a new life of hope. We are grateful that You have brought us together to bless and enrich one another's lives.

Once again, Dear Father, we are tremendously proud to be PELELIU Sailors on whom You have showered your grace so abundantly. Amen.

1982, 30 May.

God tomorrow is our Nation's Memorial Day. There was a time when people in small towns all across our land gathered in parks or cemeteries and heard flowery oratory, felt the excitement of stirring marches, stood in silence at the crack of rifles and the haunting notes of taps that spoke the Amen to the list of local heroes. All the while some elderly relative sat teary eyed on the reviewing stand. We were there to remember our Nation's history and her heroes. But that is a part of another age.

Most of us don't live in small towns anymore and high school bands no longer march five miles to stand among the graves of men they never knew. So why bother You with a prayer for Memorial Day? Because You know how badly we need a sense of heritage and destiny, at least a hero or two we can call to mind, an event that stands out because it was the point at which those values which nourish us were preserved.

We can be no greater than the men and women we most admire. So keep our memories alive with our gratitude and our gratitude alive with faithfulness. Amen.

1982, 5 June off Pattaya Beach, Thailand.

Wise and loving Father most of the men say it was great liberty -- and it was. It was great to have a break in the routine, time to relax, a variety of opportunities and experiences. It was exciting to be in an exotic land where companionship was plentiful for those who sought it amidst strange new sights and sounds and smells.

Long ago Jesus told men and women that if they would ask, seek, knock they would find. If we are bothered by what we sought and found then forgive us for the poor choice we made this time and help us to make better choices next time. Preserve us from miserable guilt which takes no pleasure in anything You have made. Help us to grow in maturity so that we may recognize what it is we are looking for in life and be able to accept it and enjoy it when we find it. In your wisdom give to each of us what he most needs and in your love enable us to recognize and receive your greatest gifts. Amen.

1982, 6 June.

Eternal God what prayer can we offer which we have not prayed before? Can we offer prayers of gratitude for the safety which has surrounded us from the beginning? Or prayers of admiration for our shipmates who continue to perform their tasks with determination and purpose? Or prayers of strength to retain stability and confidence amidst frequent changes? Or prayers of forgiveness for the times when our vision narrows or our perspective becomes distorted? On this Sunday we are particularly grateful for the renewing power of faith.

Though only a few among us find it possible to acknowledge that faith in formal worship they do so aware of their witness to others of your grace. They shine as lights and work as yeast as Jesus said they would. Their worship is an offering on behalf of all of us. For this we are glad. As they are drawn closer to You through their spiritual discipline may all our lives be enriched and blessed so that we too may become more aware of your eternal presence which sustains us now and always. Amen.

1982, 8 June.

Lord God there has been good news and bad news today. How hard it is to receive bad news and not be able to do anything about it. How natural it is to receive good news and share it. We have listened to men who were glad with the news they heard. Give them responsive shipmates to share their joy. We have listened to men whose families need them but they can only wait until the time is right to be with them. Give them patience. We have listened to men who have tried and failed and want to try again. Give them insight. We have listened to men concerned that other men be treated fairly. Give them continued concern for others. We have listened to discouraged men. Give them encouragement.

Hear again our old familiar prayer: "God grant us the courage to change those things we can change. Serenity to accept those things we cannot change; and the wisdom to know the difference." Amen.

1982, 10 June.

God we stand poised for H hour. Rehearsals and plans, preparations and coordination will be put to the test as helos and boats move hundreds of men and tons of equipment. In each of our lives there have been many H hours. There will be many more. When we have done all we can to prepare ourselves for the decisive moment help us then to trust in You for the outcome.

In all that we do keep us free from anxiety, steady in the conviction that You are our refuge and our strength, our companion and our guide. Amen.

1982, 12 June engaged in Operation Cobra Gold.

We wait at anchor Lord. Ours is a big ship and though our anchor weighs tons it is small compared to the ship it must hold firm. As the anchor holds our ship so may faith in your love hold our lives. Even though our faith may be small it has a great work to do. Let it like an anchor keep us from being tossed about and confused by every conflict or disappointment. May it keep us from drifting off in behavior which can run us aground or cause needless and dangerous collision with others. Keep us steady and secure by the anchor of trust in You. Amen.

1982, 13 June.

"The Sabbath was made for man not man for the Sabbath", Jesus said. Man needs a day set apart from the others to help keep life in perspective. Sunday doesn't need to be made an idol men worship. But men -- us, we, you and I -- need a day to remember your mighty acts, oh God, and your faithfulness: how You gave our forefathers a land in which they could make a nation, how You put within our ancestors a conviction that freedom and justice and equality of opportunity would be the basis of human community, how You made it possible for some to worship and praise You but left

all free from religious compulsion so that men who choose might be free for faith's compassions. On this Sabbath, our father, we pause for a holy moment of remembering and being grateful. Amen.

1982, 14 June.

Men for the past few days as I have gone about the ship many of you have asked, "how's the man in the hospital doing?" You didn't know his name but you were concerned about him. As most of you know by now Corporal Anthony Dewayne Valentine died shortly after two this morning. For a quarter of a century I have worked with doctors and been with families at the time of death. Never have I seen a more thoroughly professional medical team than we are blessed with on the PELELIU.

Dr. Applebaum, PELELIU'S Medical Officer and Dr. Collins, the head of the Special Surgical Unit, every doctor, nurse, and corpsman gave not only of their professional skills but lavishly of their genuine human compassion. In whatever words you form your personal prayer I hope tonight you will ask God's special presence with Corporal Valentine's family in their grief and with our medical staff. *Amen.*

1982, 15 June approaching Singapore.

The biblical poet [Ecclesiastes] wrote: There is a time for everything: a time to be born, a time to die; a time to laugh, a time to cry; a time to make love, a time to not make love; a time to speak, a time to keep quiet.

God today was payday and tomorrow we enter port. Help us to be wise enough to know what time it is. Amen.

1982, 21 June after liberty in Singapore; entering the Straits of Malacca.

God we dare not rely on our moods for there are days when for no apparent reason we are down, when we wonder at the reasons for what we do, or the place we find ourselves. Our desires are to be somewhere else. Yet, there are other days when also for no apparent reason everything is bright and if not beautiful at least there is no gnawing questioning of who, what, or where we are.

It is when we become aware of the inconstancy of our moods that we appreciate anew the constancy of your love. You are the same yesterday, today, and forever. You love us even when we don't feel very lovable. You care for us even when we could care less about who we are. We offer You our moods confident that the highs and the lows are both acceptable to You and that is good news. Amen.

1982, 23 June in the Indian Ocean.

Thank You God for inconspicuous things that brighten our days: For casual conversations with friends deeper than the words we speak, For honestly asked questions which open up thoughtful answers; For rightly timed wit turning tense situations to tolerable ones; For spontaneous congratulations offered for good news bursting to be shared; For silent sympathy more eloquent than forced words lightening sadness' shadows.

And God when such things as these are hidden grant us eyes to see and ears to hear in the spirit of him who saw men truly. Amen.

1982, 25 June crossing the Equator en-route to Diego Garcia.

Eternal God we crossed the line today. We couldn't see it but the Navigator said it was there. We believed him. It is not easy for us to believe in realities we cannot see or taste or touch. Yet much of our human life has meaning because we experience such realities as love and friendship and the bonding of men into groups.

The rite of passage from pollywog to shellback may have left us sore but the soreness will soon disappear. What will not disappear is the pride and sense of belonging to a select group of men who have crossed the Equator. In years to come we will probably embellish both the pain and the pleasure of this day. What is more important is that this visible *assault on our eyes and noses and rear ends has left a deeper invisible imprint on our lives.*

Let the invisible presence of your Holy Spirit make an equally impressive imprint on us so that we may live as brothers in your one family. Amen.

1982, 27 June approaching Diego Garcia.
Men for our prayer tonight we turn to a very old prayer written by St. Augustine when the Christian faith was very young in human history. Let us pray:

"Blessed are all thy saints my God and King who have travelled over the tempestuous sea of life and have at last made the desired port of peace and felicity. Cast a gracious eye upon us who are still in our dangerous voyage. Remember and comfort us in our distress and think of them that lie exposed to the rough storms of troubles and temptations. Strengthen our weakness that we may do valiantly in this spiritual war; help us against our own negligence and cowardice and defend us from the treachery of our unfaithful hearts. We are very frail and not very prone toward virtuous or gallant acts. Grant O Lord that we may bring our vessel safe to shore unto our desired haven. Amen."

1982, 28 June anchored off Diego Garcia.

God it is hard to know who is wetter the men in the boats or the men on the lines who have moved so much cargo today. Strengthen them we pray.

This morning we saw a rainbow off the portside of the ship while to starboard the clouds were dark and rain showers were intense. We thought of Noah and the promise and hope the rainbow held for him and his family. His world had been destroyed and everything had to begin all over again. The rainbow was a sign from You that the rebuilding would be worth all the hard work.

We also thought of Kermit the Frog and the rainbow connection. Amidst the darkness of misunderstanding or ridicule there is a beauty and symmetry where people live and work together in hope.

So whether You speak to us through Noah or Kermit may we hear your voice and see your sign and be filled with hope. Amen.

1982, 29 June departure from Diego Garcia.

Lord God we remember the story of your great servant Moses who when he grew weary in leading the people was able to continue because of the support of those beside him. Often if it were not for the strength of others who support us we would not be able to stand.

It has happened before. It will happen again. Strong and dedicated men go far beyond the ordinary in accomplishing tasks that make them very tired. If we were to single out a few we would unfortunately neglect many more. Give now to all these deserving men who have given so much to all of us in the past two days restful sleep, recovery of strength, and the satisfaction of knowing that they have again earned the admiration and praise of all of us who benefit from their arduous labors. Amen.

1982, 3 July en-route to Perth/Fremantle, Australia.

Dear Lord when men of another age sailed the vast oceans in their wooden vessels that creaked and groaned under the weight of waves and wind there were long stretches when they saw nothing but the sky and the sea.

Were they any more or any less religious than we? Did they think as often of home far away and count the days until they would hold their wives and children in their arms as we do? Did they feel the excitement of new ports eager for the anticipated pleasures based on tales of hospitality awaiting them there which they had heard from other sailors? Was there a feeling of gratitude for shipmates whose smiles were infectious or whose cheerful greetings made the days more worthwhile?

You were the same God then and we are not much different than they were. As You have favored us thus far on our journey continue to bless us so that we may be a source of strength and encouragement to one another. Amen.

1982, 4 July.

God, our Father, on this Independence Day, the 206th birthday of the Declaration of Independence, we pause for a few moments to give You thanks for a Nation conceived in liberty and dedicated to the principle that all men are endowed by their Creator with certain unalienable rights to life, liberty, and the pursuit of happiness. Life has been extended for rich and poor alike. Dread diseases that cut short human life in infancy have been virtually conquered.

Now we grapple with the killers of our technological age -- death on the highways, disorders proliferating from stressful urban existence such as heart attacks, hypertension and cancer, and the awful specter of nuclear holocaust.

In the pursuit of life help us to realize it isn't how long we live but how we live long that is important.

As a Nation we were early on convinced that we could not endure half slave and half free. No man can celebrate liberty so long as his brothers and sisters are in chains or shackled by poverty or ignorance or the denial of basic rights which enable them to contribute to the good of society while they seek their own good.

Our most elusive dream has been the pursuit of happinesss. No person can give happiness to another. It is a state which each must find for himself. Help us to discover the secret that happiness comes not in selfish pursuit of ingrown indulgence but in sharing not only what we have but who we are with one another.

Re-create in each of us the dreams of our Founding Fathers who by your grace knew that where there is no dream there can be no destiny. Amen.

1982, 6 July.

Eternal God human actions are as sure and clear as those opening notes of Beethoven's Fifth Symphony. "What a man sows that will he reap" is not just a biblical assertion: it is a law of life. There may be a long time between seed time and harvest but wheat comes from

208

wheat seeds and corn from corn and sorrow from the seeds of hate. Disruption comes from disrespect and regret from foolish disregard of the necessity of good order and discipline.

Why, oh God, does each one of us think he is the exception? We know there are exceptions and all who break the rules are not punished. But the rules break us far more often than we break them.

The cartoonist was right when he had one character say to another, "you brought it on yourself Rollo."

Grant us the moral maturity to accept responsibility for our actions to such an extent that we consider carefully what kind of seeds we want to sow since we know already that the choice of what we do determines the consequences which we bring on ourselves. Amen.

1982, 14 July engaged in Exercise Freedom Pennant.

Eternal God the prayer of the ancient Hebrew poet fashions our prayer: [Psalm 139] O Lord You have searched me and known me. You know when I lie down and when I get up. You understand me before I understand myself. You see my path clearly even while I am stumbling on my way. Before I get the words out of my mouth You have read my thoughts. You go before me and come after me and your presence is always with me. Such awareness is too wonderful for me; it is almost beyond my comprehension. Where can I go from your spirit? Or where can I ever be that You are not there already? If I fly up into the heavens You are there. If I am overcome by discouragement You wait for me in the shadows. If I get up before dawn and begin my day at the far stretches of the sea You are there. At the beginning of the long and demanding day You give me your strength. At the close of the day your peace is my rest. The brightness of the day is yours and so is the darkness of the night. How wonderful indeed, O Lord, are all your ways. So we rest ourselves in You this night with deep gratitude for the countless men whose faithful service has made it a day to remember and be glad. Amen.

1982, 16 July.

Oh Lord our great ship pitches and yaws from stern to stem and rolls from port to starboard and back again. Objects plunge unceremoniously from their usual resting places.

Our lives are like ships. We rise high with joy only to fall swiftly with sorrow. We sail smoothly along until some unexpected jolt rolls us from side to side. Experienced sailors know it is too late to secure for sea when missile hazards crash about us. Experienced voyagers on life's sea know it is too late to secure life in faith when crises shake our complacency.

As Jesus once stilled the raging waters of a turbulent sea so may your presence calm our sometimes shaky lives. Make us as eager and thorough in securing our lives in faith in your loving kindness as we are in securing our ship for sea so that we may avoid needless loss or destruction even if we cannot prevent unanticipated disturbances. Amen.

1982, 18 July.

"Holiday Routine"-- God what joyful words! They're like other words that lift our spirits; words like "Happy Birthday" or "Congratulations." They signal something special. They are welcomed when in spite of long hours and days of arduous labor men consistently give their best because they know others are counting on them.

The rhythm of work and rest was built into the structure of existence from the beginning. When You created the world You looked at what You had done and said, "That's good". Then You rested. When You delivered the children of Israel from slavery in Egypt by your chosen servant Moses You gave him the message for your people that they were to work six days then they were to rest. When Jesus was pressed on every side by incessant demands from those who saw in him your very presence he went apart for a while to rest. If the highest and best we have known valued such special times is it any wonder that we get excited when the word is passed "Now commence holiday routine"? Though we may not be too deliberate in our acknowledging the reason Lord please accept our joy as itself a prayer of gratitude. Amen.

1982, 20 July.

Lord God we pause once again for Evening Prayers aware that it is not the close of the day for many. Many among us must faithfully keep the watches of the night so essential for moving us safely, steadily, and swiftly toward our destination. Others will sleep a few hours only to be awakened to assume the mid-watch or the four-to-eight.

The life of a seafaring man is indeed a hard one. We marvel at the stamina of men who day in and night out stay steady at their assigned tasks. We marvel even more that they do so with such a positive and cheerful spirit. They exemplify the difference between tiredness and fatigue. Though we grow weary we are soon refreshed to continue and escape the oppression that would break us down.

We hear again the words of the Apostle Paul, "My grace is sufficient for your every need" [2 Corinthians 12:9] and they ring true. Renew us continually in the conviction that we may "have strength for every situation through Him who empowers us" for in His name we pray. Amen.

1982, 22 July.

Compassionate God if it were not for inspections, deadlines, and turn-overs I guess we wouldn't get nearly as much done. There is something about having to account to someone else which not only helps keep us honest but challenges us to extend ourselves a bit further. It isn't that we always intentionally let some things slide or slip up on us. Sometimes we just get so wrapped up in those things we either must do or enjoy doing that we aren't aware that we are neglecting other important matters.

It is gut-wrenching to let go of something we value greatly. The more of ourselves we have invested in it the harder it is to turn it over to someone else without anxiety.

Some of us have had the inexpressible joy of starting from the beginning. Others will take what we have created and if we have done our work well they will see our weaknesses as

213

an opportunity for improvement and will note our strengths and surpass them.

For each of us there come times for moving on -- from childhood to youth, from the civilian world to the Navy, from one assignment to another, and ultimately from this life to another.

Let us hear not only ultimately but at stages along life's way deep down within us the satisfying refrain "well done good and faithful servant enter now into the joys prepared for you." [Matthew 25:23] Amen.

1982, 24 July en-route to the Philippines.

Patient God every night at sea for more than two years Evening Prayers have been offered. Chaplains who have been with us have brought different facets of life and faith into focus before You. We are grateful for their insightful ministries.

How amazed and gratified we are at the receptiveness of the men of the PELELIU to the Evening Prayers. Sailors and Marines have listened respectfully even reverently to the prayers and commented on them. There was never any doubt that they were listening. The prayers became their prayers too -- prayers from and for the PELELIU.

While we don't know what difference it makes in each man's life we know it makes a difference for many.

When a shipmate says, "the Evening Prayer is like being tucked into bed at night," we know that as a parent cares for a child so You our Father care for us by giving us peace by your presence.

When someone says, "you know Chaplain the men in the compartment always stop and listen" we know that your word is a light to us as we walk life's way and your presence is our power.

When someone recognizes himself in the prayer and proudly acknowledges it we are glad that You know us by name and give us abundantly the things that make life worthwhile.

We shall miss this sacred moment when we no longer set out to sea. But we shall smile remembering that prayers are being faithfully offered and men of the PELELIU are expectantly listening and that each night for a moment they esteem themselves a bit more highly because they have become aware again that they are co-creators with You of a very special destiny. Amen.

1982, 25 July before reaching port in Subic Bay, the Philippines; my last night at sea on the PELELIU.

Eternal God if we were to call by name all the Toms and Tims, Jays and Jims, Marks and Mikes, Bobs and Bills,

Dons and Dougs, Genes and Georges, Jerries and Jeffs, Johns and Eds, Kens and Richs and all our other shipmates who mean so much to us what was intended as praise would become boredom. If we should limit ourselves to recounting only the major events in the short life of this magnificent ship even that would exceed the bounds of propriety.

So we simply pray, thank You God for the rare privilege of serving with so exceptional a crew on this the finest of ships. No Chaplain could have been as fortunate as I to have served with our Captain whose firm faith, personal devotion, and professional dedication have enabled his Chaplain to be what he was called to be by the grace of our Lord Jesus Christ.

May the Lord bless you all richly by His grace filling you with His love as He works within and among you doing far more than we can ask or think, for to Him be the glory, dominion and power now and evermore. Amen.

C. Prayers on Other Occasions

1. Commissioning prayers, 03 May 1980, Pascagoula, Mississippi.

Invocation:

Eternal God for as long as men have gone to sea in ships they have felt the awesome urging and mystery which takes them from those they love and to whom they long to return. For as long as men have known that life lived only for oneself is too constrictive they have taken up arms with courage to defend lives more precious than their own.

This magnificent ship brings together the Sailor's dedication to successfully sailing the unobstructed seas and the Marine's faithful tenacity in combat on land or in the air.

As the PELELIU is commissioned to take its place in our Nation's Navy we pray that those who have contributed to her planning and construction may never need have cause to be ashamed, that those whose valor is commemorated in her name may be properly honored by her outstanding service, and that those who sail her may devote themselves to the fullest accomplishment of every responsibility that is theirs.

May her nation look to her with pride as a model of excellence in execution of every task. May she be a respected adversary in conflict, an

217

effective deterrent to war, and a welcomed means of compassionate assistance to those whose misfortunes make her their means of survival and hope.

We celebrate this glorious day with deep gratitude for so significant a destiny. May we ever draw our strength and support from You whose perfect love is our peace and whose peace is our power. Amen.

Benediction:

Eternal Father from whom we come and to whom we ultimately return we commend this ship, USS PELELIU, to your care and keeping. Make her name great among those whose judgment is honored. Spread her fame throughout the land so that the young may desire to serve aboard her and the old admire her deeds.

Bless those who sail her. Sustain them always in pursuit of peace through power.

Lord bless us and keep us. Lord make your face shine upon us and be gracious to us. Lord lift up your countenance upon us and give us peace forevermore. Amen.

2. Prayer given at a Memorial Service   02 October 1980 enroute to Hawaii.

Eternal God the Source and Giver of life, the destiny toward whom all life flows, we have gathered in this memorial service to remember our shipmate Harry Selfridge. Sanctify every good memory and cut short every vain attempt to treat Harry's death lightly. In his death give us the honesty to appreciate him simply for who he was among us.

In the aweful waste of death for one so young we are dismayed at how transient and fleeting life is. Give us the grace to give to him the integrity of his death.

Comfort those who knew him well and now mourn his loss. Bring peace to the troubled spirits of all those who have courage to face their own death. Let his death be a bond between us as shipmates.

Into your care and keeping we commit ourselves for in the midst of life we are never far from death. Speak comfortingly to us so that we may need never fear the terror of death nor flee from the rare privilege of life. Amen.

3. Litany of Thanksgiving on the Second Anniversary of Commissioning, 02 May 1980 at sea.

For the shared experiences which have given a distinct character and personality to this ship,
DEAR LORD WE THANK YOU.
For the exceptional leadership and human concern which has blessed our life together,
DEAR LORD WE THANK YOU.
For safety in all our operations and for your continued protection,
DEAR LORD WE THANK YOU.
For a prevalent spirit of concern and encouragement and for the ability of men of widely varying backgrounds, temperaments, and interest to live in harmony with one another,
DEAR LORD WE THANK YOU.
For the satisfaction that has come from the successful accomplishment of every assigned task and the wholesome pride which this has engendered,
DEAR LORD WE THANK YOU.
On this the second anniversary of the commissioning of USS PELELIU we rejoice in a brief but glorious past. We thank You for the strength and determination to meet the challenges of the present. And we seek renewed devotion to faithfulness to You and to one another in the approaching future. Amen.

4. From a Memorial Observance of Dr. Martin Luther King's birthday 15 January 1982. A Litany of the American Dream (composed of excerpts from Dr. King's speech at Lincoln University, Pennsylvania 06 June 1961 when he received an honorary Doctor of Law degree).

MARTIN LUTHER KING, JR. WAS A DREAMER WHO SAID:

America is essentially a dream, a dream as yet unfulfilled. It is a dream of a land where men of all races, of all nationalities, and of all creeds can live together as brothers.

HE WAS A DREAMER WHO BELIEVED:

The substance of the dream is expressed in these sublime words, words lifted to cosmic proportions: 'We hold these truths to be self-evident that all men are created equal, that they are endowed by the Creator with certain unalienable rights, that among these are life, liberty, and the pursuit of happiness.' This is the dream.

HE WAS A DREAMER WHO INSISTED:

It does not say some men, but it says all men. It does not say all white men, but it says all men, which includes black men. It does not say all Gentiles, but it says all men, which includes Jews. It does not say all Protestants, but it says all men which includes Catholics.

HE WAS A DREAMER WHO WARNED:

The hour is late. The clock of destiny is ticking out. It is trite, but urgently true, that if America is to remain a first-class nation she can no longer have second-class citizens.

HE WAS A DREAMER WHO CHALLENGED:
The American Dream will not become a reality devoid of the larger dream of a world brotherhood and peace and good will. Through our scientific genius we have made of this world a neighborhood. Now through our moral and spiritual development we must make of it a brotherhood. In a real sense we must learn to live together as brothers or we will all perish together as fools.

HE WAS A DREAMER WHO OBSERVED:
I can never be what I ought to be until you are what you ought to be. You can never be what you ought to be until I am what I ought to be.

HE WAS A DREAMER WHO FEARED:
The great problem confronting us today is that we have allowed the means by which we live to outdistance the ends for which we live. We have allowed our civilization to outrun our culture and so we are in danger now of ending up with guided missiles in the hands of misguided men.

HE WAS A DREAMER WHO PROCLAIMED:
If we are to implement the American Dream we must get rid of the notion once and for all that there are superior and inferior races. This means that members of minority groups must make

it clear that they can use their resources even under adverse circumstances. We must make full and constructive use of the freedom we already possess. We must not use our oppression as an excuse for mediocrity and laziness.

HE WAS A DREAMER WHO KNEW WHAT IS REQUIRED:

We need religion and education to change attitudes and to change the hearts of men. We need legislation and federal action to control behavior. It may be true that the law can't make a man love me but it can keep him from lynching me and I think that's pretty important also.

HE WAS A DREAMER WITH A VISION OF FAITH:

Black supremacy is as dangerous as white supremacy and God is not interested merely in the freedom of black men and brown men and yellow men. God is interested in the freedom of the whole human race and in the creation of a society where all men can live together as brothers, where every man will respect the dignity and the worth of human personality.

HE WAS A DREAMER WHO SAW A NEW DAY DAWNING:

That will be the day when all of God's children black men and white men, Jews and Gentiles, Catholics and Protestants will be able to join hands and sing in

the words of the Old Negro Spiritual, 'Free at last! Free at last! Thank God Almighty, we are free at last!'
THANK GOD MARTIN LUTHER KING, JR. WAS A DREAMER.
AMEN.

5. Verse to the Navy Hymn composed for a wedding.

Several wedding ceremonies were performed while I was attached to the PELELIU. The wedding ceremony which I used during my Naval career will appear in *Volume III: Prayers of a Navy Chaplain ashore.*

I composed a verse for the ceremony of one of the officers and his fiancee at the Chapel, Naval Station Treasure Island, San Francisco, CA.

> *Eternal God whose love creates*
> *Bless these whose vows we celebrate.*
> *Enrich their joys with love impressed*
> *Sustain them in life's deep distress.*
> *O grant that in Thine own good will*
> *True marriages may be fulfilled.*

6. Other occasions.

There were numerous other occasions when prayer was offered. Many of those prayers were extemporaneous and not written down or recorded. Some of the prayers that were written for those occasions have been misplaced or lost.

There were prayers at weddings and funerals. There were prayers at christenings and baptisms. There were prayers on the mess decks for birthdays and anniversaries always with delicious cake from the ship's galley. There were prayers at Wives Club meetings and Ombudspersons meetings. There were prayers when we had guests aboard. There were prayers in the Chaplain's Office as the Chaplain and one of the crew struggled with some issue or problem which needed resolving, or news of great sorrow or death had been delivered.

These too were Sacred Moments which enriched and blessed our lives.

The title of the three volumes is taken from the prayer given on 24 July 1982 two nights before we reached Subic Bay, the Philippines and my detachment from the PELELIU. I affirm now what I said then. "We shall miss this sacred moment when we no longer set out to sea."

Chapter III.
Another Ship, another time.

During my service as a Navy Chaplain I often had occasion to hold worship services aboard ships other than the one to which I was assigned. Whenever there was a ship in port Yokosuka that requested the services of a Chaplain for worship and I was available I was honored to go aboard. There were several destroyers on WESTPACS and there were supply ships in port for replenishing.

I have included this last section of Evening Prayers aboard USS TOWERS (DDG 9) because I thought going to sea aboard her would be my last opportunity to go to sea since I was based at CFAY and ministering at the Chapel of Hope. Little did I know, or anyone else for that matter at the time, that I would be assigned to a second tour as Command Chaplain on the MIDWAY (CV 41) to close out my career.

The Captain, Executive Officer and Command Master Chief made me feel right at home, even accompanying me and several of the crew to some of the orphanages and the TB hospital near Chinhae, Korea which I had visited often when I was a member of the staff of COMDESRON FIFTEEN more than a decade before.

1988, 07 December en-route from Yokosuka, Japan to Pusan, Korea.

Good evening men. This is Chaplain Murphey. Being with you on this voyage to Korea is the answer to a prayer, the fulfillment of a dream. Some of the most impressive experiences of my life have been with the orphanages, hospitals, and old-folks homes in and around Chinhae. I am so excited that you and I are going to see them on Monday.

We will take some candy and fruit, but the best gift of all will be that we take ourselves to share with them. I am repeatedly amazed and gratified at the kindness and generosity of you, the American Sailor. You are a wonderful company of men. If I can serve you by visiting with you or sharing in Bible Study or Spiritual Ops let me know. I'm in the Unit Commander's Stateroom. Now let us pray.

Eternal God, thanks once again for this sacred experience of going to sea. Here upon the immense ocean we get a new sense of perspective. Here we come to realize how dependent we are on one another. Here we gain appreciation for the beauty of your creation: a fiery red sunset, a floating snow-covered mountain, a deep blue constant sea.

Here we experience a friendly greeting, a kind response, a courteous acceptance. Grant now the reward of restful sleep to those whose work is done for the day. To our watch-standers grant the alert vigilance of those in whose hands is our safety and well-being, sustained by your eternal strength and presence. Amen.

1988, 08 December.

Eternal God, life's ordinary experiences sometimes become the means by which we become aware of your extraordinary presence in our lives. We have seen You at work among us today.

We watched a man instruct a shipmate in a way that recognized his shipmate's intelligence and dignity as he passed on to him essential knowledge.

We saw a Chief patiently and with good humor pass on his knowledge and experience to new men eager to learn of life at sea.

We listened as an Officer quietly asked a question of a seaman in such a way that he was able to learn a lesson he will never forget.

We saw and heard so much more but in it all You were at work. We thank You for your Spirit at work in and among us enabling us to know and do your will. May we grow in our ability to express your extra-ordinary presence in our ordinary lives. Amen.

1988, 09 December.

Lord God, this has not been a good day for many of us. For some it was their first battle with a new enemy -- seasickness. For others it was a return engagement which doesn't seem to get much better. Yet, sick as we were, we believed we would eventually win out. There are illnesses from which we don't recover so quickly; our Captain cautioned us against one today.

Our Command Master Chief shared with me tonight the news that one of our shipmates -- Electricians Mate Chief Petty Officer Emanuel Antolin is on the very seriously ill list with poor prognosis in Tripler Hospital, Hawaii. We pray for him, his wife and their children and other family members. We pray for those who care for their needs whether as doctors, nurses, corpsmen, or child caregivers. Sustain Chief Antolin and his family by the assurance of your eternal presence. Grant compassion equal to their professional skills for those who care for him and his family.

And, God, as we enter Pusan tomorrow may we also look out for one another, so that the memories we leave with will be even better than the excited anticipation we have now of getting there. Amen.

1988, 13 December en-route from Pusan, Korea to Yokosuka, Japan.

Tonight before the Evening Prayer, I want to personally thank our Skipper, Captain Baer, our XO, Commander Tully, and our Command Master Chief Moore for their outstanding support of yesterday's visit to Chinhae. I would like to mention all 28 TOWERS men who went but I won't do that; you know who you are. Though we had only a brief time at the hospital and orphanages, I assure you it was enough that you will never be quite the same because of it. Now let us pray:

Eternal God, the experiences of the past few days in Pusan have become a part of our personal history. For some the memories will last a life-time and they will be drawn from time to time to the Land of the Morning Calm and its beautifully industrious and friendly people.

We gained a new appreciation for our own families and Country. A new awareness comes to us that You are the Creator God and Father of all peoples everywhere. If we disappointed ourselves or did things which cause us guilt or shame forgive us. Assure us of your love which enables us to become co-creators with You of our destiny so that we may in time become the kind of men you have created us to be. Amen.

1988, 14 December en-route from Pusan, Korea to Yokosuka, Japan.

A novelist once wrote, "A man's biography ought to be written from his death backwards." [Jean Paul] There is truth in that, especially for his family and friends. News of someone's death meets with different reactions. The better we know the person who has died the more two things happen: one is that we want a quiet time and place to express to God our disbelief, anger, and sorrow, the other is that we want to get with someone else who knew him and talk about him with each other.

On any ship few days go by without someone getting news of a person they love being seriously ill or having died. Today on the TOWERS BTFN Jones learned of his close relative's death. Later in the day, the Captain broke the news to all of us of Chief Antolin's untimely death.

Years ago a death was announced by ringing, or tolling, a bell slowly. John Donne, the English poet asked the question which Ernest Hemingway made famous, "For whom does the bell toll"? The answer is that the news of any person's death, particularly someone whose life has been a part of my life leaves me saddened because he is no longer a part of the things we shared together. It also reminds me that someday the bell will toll for me.

Our lives and our deaths are in God's hands, so tonight we share a poem that has comforted people in life and in death for about three thousand years. May God speak to us through the Twenty-third Psalm as He has to so many, so often before:

The Lord is my Shepherd, I shall not want.

He makes me lie down in green pastures;

He leads me beside still water;

He restores my soul.

He leads me in right paths for his name's sake.

Even though I walk through the darkest valley,

I fear no evil for You are with me;

Your rod and your staff -- they comfort me.

You prepare a table before me in the presence of my enemies;

You anoint my head with oil; my cup overflows.

Surely goodness and mercy shall follow me all the days of my life.

And I shall dwell in the house of the Lord my whole life long. Amen.

Conclusion

It is time to bring these Sacred Moments to a close. In bringing them together memories have flooded in of those times and places and especially those persons with whom they were shared. I never ceased to be amazed that the men on those ships were so attentive to the Evening Prayers at Sea.

When the PELELIU published its first *Cruise Book* covering the time from its Commisioning through its first WESTPAC the editor was gracious enough to put this caption with my picture:

Chaplain Paul W. Murphey, LCDR, CHC, was ship's Chaplain from commissioning until his departure for the Naval Submarine Base, Bangor, Washington in August, 1982. A former college professor, Chaplain Murphey was a familiar face - and voice - to all PELELIU crewmen. His evening prayer, offered each night at sea, was a time-honored Navy tradition that was anticipated and appreciated by the crew.

I am deeply grateful for the honor given me of serving the men of COMDESRON FIFTEEN (CDS 15) and USS PELELIU (LHA 5) and have the hope that if any of them pick up this volume and browse through it they will find some fond memories of those days and nights at sea together. Should they want to they may contact me at pwmurphey@wavecable.com or 12162 Country Meadows LN NW, Silverdale, WA 98383.

I have deliberately tried to stay away from anything derogatory either in my personal affairs or the lives of the crews of the ships I served. I believed it would serve no good purpose and would detract from the value of these Sacred Moments.

I apologize in advance if someone looks for his name and doesn't find it. I have tried to be judicious in the names given and regret being unable to include that entire company of men and women who were also so much a part of my life.

I turn now to compiling the next volume in this three volume set: *Sacred Moments – Prayers of a Navy Chaplain at Sea aboard USS MIDWAY (CV 41).*

I intend to follow that with volume three: *Sacred Moments – Prayers of a Navy Chaplain Ashore* including prayers from my Inactive Reserve duty through the first few years of my retirement.

About the Author

Paul Warren Murphey retired from the U.S. Naval Reserve, Chaplain Corps as a Commander, in January 1992.

After eleven years as Professor of Religion and Director of the Interdisciplinary Humanities Program, Transylvania University he went on Active Duty at the age of 44. The last seven of those years he was a Naval Reserve Chaplain serving the Navy and Marine Corps Reserve Center, Lexington, KY. His teaching career had begun at Eureka College, IL where he was College Chaplain and Assistant Professor of History for five years.

Duty assignments were: COMDESRON FIFTEEN (CDS 15), Yokosuka, Japan, 1976-78; FIRST FORCE SERVICE SUPPORT GROUP (1st FSSG), Camp Pendleton, CA, 1978-80;USS PELELIU (LHA 5), Long Beach, CA, 1980-82; NAVAL SUBMARINE BASE, Bangor, WA, 1982-85; USS MIDWAY (CV41), Yokosuka, Japan, 1985-87; COMMANDER FLEET ACTIVITIES YOKOSUKA (CFAY), Chapel of Hope, 1987-90; USS MIDWAY (CV 41), Yokosuka, Japan, 1990-91. His awards include Meritorious Service Medal with gold star and Navy Commendation Medal with two gold stars.

His BA is from Texas Christian University, M.Div. from Vanderbilt Divinity School, M.S.L.S. from the University of Kentucky, M.B.A. from City University of Seattle, and Ph.D. degree from Vanderbilt University. He is listed in *Who's Who in America*, 2012 edition.

13922936R00147

Made in the USA
San Bernardino, CA
09 August 2014